differences of success

introduction

book about life and the portrait of success stories of the three leaders. who changed the world, the idea seems crazy, but more effective expectations. to achieve all that they are people who dare to dare to think, and for the sake of passion and desire to work in a passion. deduct from successes in life brought little benefit to everyone and the whole world with their passion.

while composing with words if you use inappropriate or wrong please forgive. or contact via email nguyenthuan190@yahoo.com authors thank the support and attention of the readers.

nguyenthuan

Portrait from Life

Life sometimes makes us think, what we need? and what to do? How much is enough and how much is not enough for a human life I would like to share with you what I'm looking for and have done for my life.

born and raised in a family is quite normal, can also be called a normal life because of my childhood deprivation are not thinking in my humble view. I've matured and grown up in his thinking, from childhood I have many dreams for my future life, I wish I were not your parents, I wish I could make more money I wish I met someone and they'll give me some real big money to serve the life I dreamed of. I thought I could live in a dream, then I think that one day their dream will come true. knowing where a miracle occurs, then your dream and I would come true. I will always wait for it to me as a miracle. you know?at the worst defeat I feel I must be very confident because there are something like the bed waiting for me ahead. one thing that maybe now I realize that there is anything that will come to you if you do not really try.

I was now going to work pretty well is normal as my life, I worked for a small restaurant in a city that way about 130 miles of my house. The first months of work but I get paid little. I have to send the money to take care subsidies parents because now my family have lived in the same salary that I was little. return to the moon every night I could not sleep I can, and not as I do not think finding ways to make money so much and so fast, it was under my thoughts seem to be more of a life but it has to be with me? I started to know about the internet as an entertainment tool, I hope that someday I will not think what nonsense but I did not do all that. thanks to the internet I learned more from playing games, reading newspapers, watching news, and now I have discovered that from so long I never thought about is making money thanks to the internet. but as I know there are many billionaires have just changed my life thanks to the internet game. I began work of their money and expect life changed thanks to the internet, I search and follow the instructions of the post from the forum, which is making money with internet, work with the internet, making money ... v ... v.. , And these words are also commonly used search terms as I sit on the computer. I follow the instructions to register as members of a certain site and receive their email every day, every email as up from 1-5 dollars they paid me when the threshold payment they require the real number is 1000 usd dizziness. if an email received 1-5 usd 1000 usd payment threshold, the story is very near, not far from my wish for such things as before. I make a lot of accounts involved so many different sites with the desire to make more money and become rich quickly. I also post my article on the forums to develop a network of its members. at the request of the site I joined, I have to develop a network of members, which means I have to introduce more people to participate as a member for that site in the form of my subordinates in order to receive commissions from the introduction and development of its network. I seem to do very well in this work to my team members grow very fast. but the email that I received it a few days a month I did not even get email at all. I contact the administrator does not see a reply that is only getting a lot of junk email. amount to 1000 dollars threshold payment will never come to me. but I never give up and will never never give up. I think a reputable site, but there are also sites that do not hold credibility because if they do not have the people get rich from the internet?

I think so and went to find another way to register other sites that I think is a reputable long as the amount they promised to pay me real high. because to think they could not have gotten my interest when.

Lessons of life

if you have been the same thoughts as I look back so you've lived and worked really think of yourself? I've been through many trials of life which help me have more confidence than from life.

Quick steps on industry money on the internet I had stumbled so many times to achieve success. until one day I received an email of her Mrs. Marilyn. Z. Gloucester

I believe that my life has changed. why I have such thoughts? because according to her promise, she was in bed sick with a cancer in the last period. Her husband died several years ago, her son is not going to find someone to trust the trust property that she and her husband had created in the past. I do not know where she has information about me and I do not care about her I read her email, but please feel dives. I just like going to a different world a world of promise. Her email content below.

With Honor.

I will Introduce myself as
Mrs. Marilyn. Z. Gloucester. Originally I am
from United State, I spent all my life here with my
Husband Late in Ghana
Were he was Gold Dealer. I am a dying woman 78 years old and was diagnosed
for Kidney (Renal Cell) Cancer about four years ago, after the ngay
death of my husband, I have been touched to donate

inherited from my late husband for the good work of Charities, rather than
His allow relatives to use my husband's hard earned fund. As I lay on my
sick bed, I want you to help me in Carrying out my last wish on earth

that will very profitable to you. I want to WILL a total sum of $ 5.7
million dollars to you that I Want You to Distribute part to any charity
homes around you especially for me Most Country, please for Further
my contact information as soon as you th? Attorney.

with theLawyer details:
Barrister. John Hagee
Attorney at-Law.
J. Hagee & Associates LLP
11 Staple Inn Buildings, WC1V 7QH Accra.
Email: Attorney_solicitor@consultant.com
Tel: 233-265-488-320

Regards,
Marilyn Zaini Gloucester.

As you can guess I'll have to do with her request? but when confronted with a proposal so I'm sure that no one can escape temptation. as my action is now required to listen and follow her. I do not need to think much just a phone call to the lawyer that she has requested. through conversation that the more I trust her, as I have discussed with her attorney and he did not ask me anything just ask me to give him my full name and address of the household my projection. as well as my bank information so he could complete the procedure from his bank. and of course the completion of the procedure on the number of her assets will be transferred into my bank account as an inheritance. I also had several talks with her attorney and contact the bank that she gave me. I received a request from banks but this is not to provide information as before, but they asked me to pay an activation fee before her account was transferred to me. 2500 usd fee I have to consider very carefully before deciding last few days and I also contacted her lawyer. My guiding fee payment to the bank so I can receive her inheritance fast. he was very happy and enthusiastic is a great man I ever met, I want to tell him that I would love him to this lifetime. I will deliver him what he requested, including the activation fee so he could help me complete the dossier. again I pray that god the supreme god to protect him and her, looking forward to any peace with them.

It is a belief that this ancient faith in me I never have been believed for a promise. for me the money 2500 usd is not a small figure but I would add that I set out from their faith.because they were brought to light in my life who will help me realize the dream, who will bring my wealth I silently thank them because they helped me. I believe in them only because they will help me change my life. last heard you think it is completely sugar? but for me it was true the fact that no one lies.

You do not ever believe in me and I would not trust anybody to anyone. because I finally realized what we were waiting for a totally not in the best of my park now seems to break when I realized I had a goal. after receiving the activation fee I have sent them, I just wait and get what I get is a lesson. waiting for an answer from them even a question, please let me know a quote that I was fooled, so can also make me realize that I was awake and I'm also a little intelligence to know just being lazy a lazy game that later when I learned to call it trick technology.

With life challenges

life sometimes we will have to face difficulties. and I dare to believe that no one among us has not stumbled once, not once encountered difficulties. the fall of the main difficulties that will help us understand more about life.

will help us get the lessons I call it a lesson of life. from those lessons will be learned from his experience of life that I believe nothing more valuable that experience.

to be successful you first have to accept that people know what will come with the card. accept defeat, to take risks, accept challenges will bring you success does not have anything in the world come to you naturally without a tradeoff. to be successful you must trade with failure. to get better tomorrow you have to build for life today, what would you do today to get tomorrow? please do not ever ask me because for me it's a pretty tough question. but for me, I am ready to accept the challenge I had to pay for what he did. after years of training and learning seemed to have little understanding of the work, with current job and I'm holding the position is also difficult to reach anyone at my age. working in a restaurant is quite popular and the number of tourists from very large to say, but for me the work is not all what I need is to learn and train themselves the creativity and inspiration proud. if you're standing in a position that successful people have money, fame, power that you dare to take on new challenges for my life? I'm not asking you to give everything I have but I just want to challenge you in a new location for a new job. it will help you a lot less because you can see again my life can you learn from the experience of living and experience the new environment.

all that is true because many people have succeeded

because they dared to challenge the failure. to achieve success you must learn to accept challenges and cope with failure. How then can you be successful, but when you know how to use his success to serve little benefit for everyone is that success will become greater. a success that brought little benefit to people you will get very many, up to this point, perhaps no one knows about microsoft software used for browsing. and any computer that does not need this software. Bill Gates, a hero of the internet a master switch software, I say that because no one can reap much success as his wealth and his strong will also be shared with people of all time and every generation. you take a look what he has done for mankind? His main success could change the human race so why you can not do it like him? because your success is taking but not giving, but for him to get into the right to go first. you made less any benefit to mankind yet? if you succeed on taking your success is only temporary. because that is your own, give or receive this question many people have asked me, but until now, I still have not found any suitable answers. you can give me some advice as advice for you, I'll have to do to achieve what I want? trust and take the wait How much for my expectations? simply a lesson for life, but I've been through because I still trust in my people for so long from now still believe that someday I will be rich. but not a success in life that I want this wealth is the giving away of someone. heard was crazy but I'm still waiting for that one day someone told me that they're going to find me, God gave them a few years they've met me. and they will give me what they have to do it a home they own, a property that many nights I dream can not think of any. I met them and was willing to let me do all what they have, without any exchange that took place between me and them what they see, I just do what they have just played only a recipient role. with an introduction to international money transfer service someone has used this service and transfer money overseas, do not know why I'm lucky or something by mistake that people get that money and recipient's name as me. but because of a delay taking that made my money can not arrive at my place, it is one thing more. they have done so much to relate to me but now that amount of time has passed to the recipient. they also can not return because the person who transferred the money has not yet died a month ago. they are waiting for a request from me and they will do all I can to get that money is mine now. I will have to give them all the information about me and will send them a copy after my international passport, they accept both scans are required to send via email for quick and convenient services in a knife. I forgot to say that they have to contact me via email that I know all about them just how much of it. but what they know about me a lot appears to be complete, I feel very confident they know where someone may have mistakenly called my animal? or are due to Mrs. Marilyn. Z. Gloucester moved me that I was wrongly suspected her again I feel sorry for a woman who I was waiting. I pray that she is going to heaven and will be the protection of God, as she was protecting me. but with e-mail content so I did not trust myself anymore, because it seems like I've lost faith in it then.

Welcome to Western Union
Western Union Money Transfer Outlet
Outlet Manager: Mr. Ben Paul

Ref: WYN9201DL0.
Authorization code: TWH82MQ012
Shop register code: 836QDHK92.

M.T.C.N Number: 017-591-6070

ACKNOWLEDGEMENT OF WESTERN UNION STATUS
transaction.

Yes, you have an outstanding payment with the Western Union Money Transfer Office, sent from Lagos, Nigeria in regards to compensate on the past you had with the Nigerian Experience scamers. This is been sponsored by the Nigerian Government and done in collaboration with the World Bank and Western Union Money Transfer.

Your first transfer of U.S. $ 10,000 from a total sum of $ 250,000 that been awarded to you is ready for pick up in any Western Union outlet close to you pending When you activate your transfer because this payment has been online for close to 2months and was first emailed to you by the Regional Manager Mrs. Benita Osagie.

Western Union Money Transfer has instructed that your payment should not be activated yet your payment file because the need will be renewed before it released to

you for your first daily pick up of U.S. $ 10,000.
The Mandatory renewal of your payment file Usd Will
cost $ 795:00 only.

Main reason why the activation of your payment for the
transfer has to be made is because often allow Nigeria to
transfer funds out of the country and in a case whereby
this outlet has been Authorized to do so, has any
payment to be received out Issued within a period of
21days and if not received within that period of time, an
activation fee must paid before the receiver could have
picked it up.

I advise that you locate any Western Union Money
Transfer Office close to you and make the payment of $
795:00 over that WE CAN finalize everything for you to
start the pick-up of your U.S. $ 10,000 daily.

Below is an information in you required to make the
payment.

Name: Bruce Malawy

Address: Edo State Nigeria.

After you have made the transfer, you are to make sure
that the below information is sent to me via email:

Sender's Name:
Sender's Address:

MTCN (Money Transfer Control Number):
Question And Answer Text:

As soon as the activation of your payment for the transfer of U.S. $ 10,000.00 is made you will be able to visit the nearest Western Union outlet close to you and confirm the payment and be able to have it picked up.

Thanks for your Understanding and co-operation in this issue.

Regards
Paul Mr.Ben
Outlet Manager
Western Union Money Transfer Outlet.

NOTE: DO NOT DISCLOSE YOUR MTCN OUT YOUR TOTAL UNTIL YOU FINALLY WITHDRAW FUNDS FROM THE WESTERN UNION MONEY TRANSFER OFFICE, THIS IS VERY IMPORTANT.

for me now I've lost confidence in. but I'm still waiting for a something, one is completely true that it is successful.

Success stories

The story of the founder of Amazon.com Company

As founder and chief executive officer of Amazon.com, Jeff Bezos current owners of property clause 2 to $ 9 billion. He is the son of Miguel Mike Bezos, chief executive of Exxon Corporation and Jacklyn Gise Bezos, Bezos has always maintained close relationships with boys and girls.

In 14 years, Bezos has dreamed of becoming a cosmonaut or a physicist, a grandfather, his dream was kindled because he is the manager of the Nuclear Energy Commission. With this ambition, Bezos has studied the science projects and engineering that had piled up in warehouses of their parents.

Passion for science was revealed when he was making kaleidoscope, where users can view an image in the world want it. This story can be found in a book Turning On Bright Minds: A Parent Looks at Gifted Education in Texas. Bezos was on holiday for years at his grandfather's ranch in Cotulla, Texas, when he was practicing his skills in mechanical windmills fixing and doing odd jobs.

After graduating from Palmetto High School, where he was elected class president and a representative of the entire school, he continued to learn about electrical and information technology at Princeton University. In 1986, Bezos attended FITEL, a high technology company in New York. 2 years later, Bezos began working at the Trust Company bank in New York, where he operated the computer systems developed and became the youngest vice president of the company in 1990.

Vice President is the first important position in the career of Bezos. Bezos worked for the company D.E. Shaw & Co. in New York from 1990 to 1994, and helped build one of the most complex reserve fund on Wall Street. In 1992, Bezos became the youngest vice president of the company.

Interested customers, not competitors, that is our business motto of "obsession" current Bezos - Amazon.com. He discovered the growth potential of the Internet. He and his wife (novelist) moved to Seattle and sowed the first seeds for Amazon.com from renting apartments in their suburbs.

Before conducting business on the Internet, Bezos and his team work took years to develop a program for database and build websites that sell books, music and video on the Internet. Although the company's profit is number 0, because all earnings are spent on marketing and buying other companies, but Amazon.com accomplishments achieved enormous:

* Defeat Sears on capital value on the market, with $ 17

billion in 1998.
* Shares of Amazon.com posted to the public from May 1997 on the NASDAQ stock market. Many workers have conducted their business and now shares have become millionaires.
* Currently the online store is the world's largest, with sales of 1.92 billion dollars in 2000.
* Over 60,000 sites are connected with Amazon.com
* Bezos is known as a fan of science fiction, a man witty, gregarious, interested in anything that can be revolutionized by computers and has a special tone cheery smile. Indeed, he has much good to laugh and rejoice.

The story of the father of google.

If all the world like Google and use it as a body of work with the Internet, not many people know that the founder of this huge site from Russia.
When 5 years old, Sergey Brin and his family to leave Russia to settle in America. 25 years later, a dynamic young man with a permanent smile on your lips have

become a major symbol of Silicon Valley is full of public people who made the revolution of information technology great 10 years ago.

Sergey's father, Mikhail Brin capital is a math teacher in high school in Moscow. As to America, he taught at the University of Maryland. Sergey's mother worked in the aerospace agency U.S. - NASA. Bathed in atmosphere science, Sergey express mathematical skills and passion from very early electronics. When first grade, his teacher suggested to the printing processing method, a very practical invention when the computer industry began entering American homes. High school graduate, Sergey in Mathematics from the University of Maryland and obtained undergraduate degree with honors and scholarships from Stanford University. At the new school, he plans to learn Russian origin straight to PhD. However, his study has been left undone by the crazy idea.

Sergey has a special passion for the Internet and see it as the way forward for humanity in the future. As also in college, he built a search engine oriented HTML, the predecessor of the current Google. Later, Sergey developed a software copyright protection network, a site assessment quality movies and a few websites with premium features other Vietnamese. Time, Sergey met Larry Page of Stanford University and a project has been two young and ambitious romantic draw. After making sketches, both went for the donors but also where they receive only ones shaken by most corporate networks at that time agreed that Google is the product of utopian minds. Then the efforts of two people searching finally paid off with a nod of his charismatic Andy Bechtolsheim, founder of Sun Micro Systems and Granite Systems. So is the idea of Sergey and Larry just as the plane was going to be a runway, waiting on takeoff. Recognizing the feasibility of the idea of two boys. Bechlotsheim has poured $ 25 million on the website called www.google.com.

Said that a website may sound simple, but actually Google is a giant machine. After its inception in 1998, with the advantages of their Vietnam, Google has grown rapidly as blowing, became a popular Internet addresses leading. In 2000, when Google come a new contract with "big" Yahoo, allowing two giants on the website of each search query. Handshake with Yahoo makes Google becomes more famous. However, it is essential to bring the Google boom is that the super features of its Vietnamese.

The office of Chairman of the board of Google Eric Schmidt, a man full of skill and experience. Sergey is also chief technology officer Larry is director of product management. Sergey and Larry were not even hold a doctorate when they left Stanford to pursue his project. But now, under the management of them is more than 100 doctors and 2,000 other senior staff. Google's search engine now includes more than 10,000 powerful computer.

Earlier this year, Google added to its list of search 1 billion Web sites, reached 4.28 billion web addresses. Before the rise of Google, Yahoo has seen in this competition a real threat. So in 2003, Yahoo has invested $ 2 billion to upgrade their systems. Then also launched search engine independent, not dependent on Google. From the idea of two young students, Google has now become a huge company. Sergey's fortune is also increasingly bloated. According to Forbes, the man of Russian origin, owns about $ 4 billion.

As one of the companies of the world's most powerful Internet, Google is where the work environment very pleasant. Company employees serving coffee, wine and free meals. They can bring their children to work and can optionally use 20% of work time on other things. This, according to Google executives, who can help to promote creativity.

Google: pay attention to the impossible.

It is a story about the success of the two really strange young man Larry Page and Sergey Brin - the founders of Google. Only with their minds, in a mere six years they have become billionaires.

Google's success is the success of these wonderful ideas and creativity. "Take care not possible, try to do what most people do not think" - the motto of the founders of Google has taken the future direction of Google:

Larry Page and Sergey Brin into loud cheers in the hall of excited young people growing up often do when greeting the rock star. Casual dress, they sat down and smiled very fresh. "Do you know the story of Google? Do you want me to tell you not heard? "- Page asked. "Yes" - the crowd shouted foul lon.Mo and tears up 99%

That was on May 9-2003, hundreds of students and faculty in an Israeli high school attended to hear the super mathematical minds Vietnam, the young inventor to speak.

Many of them like Brin, because they too far from his family in Russia to look to America. And their enthusiasm shows in Page when Page starred in pairs to create a powerful information tool and easy to use most of their time

- A tool for change has spread like fire throughout the world. Like kids playing basketball and dreamed of becoming a Michael Jordan, these students wanted to be like Sergey Brin and Larry Page a day.
-
Opening page: "Google was founded when Brin and I'm doing a doctorate in computer science at Stanford University. We do not know exactly what I wanted to do. I have every crazy idea is to download everything available online to their PC. I told my instructor that it only takes a week. I've downloaded are a part of what is on something that takes about a year. " All the students laughed big. Page continued: "There is an expression I

search engine independent, not dependent on Google. From the idea of two young students, Google has now become a huge company. Sergey's fortune is also increasingly bloated. According to Forbes, the man of Russian origin, owns about $ 4 billion.

As one of the companies of the world's most powerful Internet, Google is where the work environment very pleasant. Company employees serving coffee, wine and free meals. They can bring their children to work and can optionally use 20% of work time on other things. This, according to Google executives, who can help to promote creativity.

Google: pay attention to the impossible.

It is a story about the success of the two really strange young man Larry Page and Sergey Brin - the founders of Google. Only with their minds, in a mere six years they have become billionaires.

Google's success is the success of these wonderful ideas and creativity. "Take care not possible, try to do what most people do not think" - the motto of the founders of Google has taken the future direction of Google:

Larry Page and Sergey Brin into loud cheers in the hall of excited young people growing up often do when greeting the rock star. Casual dress, they sat down and smiled very fresh. "Do you know the story of Google? Do you want me to tell you not heard? "- Page asked. "Yes" - the crowd shouted foul lon.Mo and tears up 99%

That was on May 9-2003, hundreds of students and faculty in an Israeli high school attended to hear the super mathematical minds Vietnam, the young inventor to speak.

Many of them like Brin, because they too far from his family in Russia to look to America. And their enthusiasm shows in Page when Page starred in pairs to create a powerful information tool and easy to use most of their time

- A tool for change has spread like fire throughout the world. Like kids playing basketball and dreamed of becoming a Michael Jordan, these students wanted to be like Sergey Brin and Larry Page a day.
-
Opening page: "Google was founded when Brin and I'm doing a doctorate in computer science at Stanford University. We do not know exactly what I wanted to do. I have every crazy idea is to download everything available online to their PC. I told my instructor that it only takes a week. I've downloaded are a part of what is on something that takes about a year. " All the students laughed big. Page continued: "There is an expression I

learned in college, it's just impossible to care. It is an expression or. You should try to do what most people may think. "

In the history of invention and thick glasses of capitalist America, no one has succeeded as fast as them. Thomas Edison took half a century to invent the light bulb, Alexander Graham Bell to take many years to invent and improve the phone, right next decade tens of hard hard work, Henry Ford created a new the assembly line and turn it into a modern industry of automobile production and consumption, while Thomas Watson "child" had to work very hard for many years until IBM to manufacture the modern computer. But Brin and Page, just six years, received graduate research project and turn it into a global business worth billions of dollars. Page continued to tell the glory days of two people: "When we first met, everyone thought the other person's frustrating. But then we pass it and sometimes you become good. It was a time eight years ago. Then we really started to work. " He emphasized this important point: although the idea but the sweat and tears accounted for 99%. Page said: "This is a valuable lesson for us. We did not mention the holidays, forget the bright and dark. We had to work hard and a lot of effort. "

Page also wanted to convey something more: inspiration. Page said: "I grew up without the Internet, or its current form and its global network. Today, the world has changed a lot because you are in a position to collect information on any subject matter in the world. And this is extremely different from the time I was at school. " Brin then added: "You have many strengths that we have no generation. These will help you succeed earlier in life than us. "

Career just started.

Brin and Page finished their stories and motioned for the crowd of students now is the time to ask questions. "You think Google has marked the career of yours?" - The first question posed to Brin and Page. Brin answered, "I think it's the smallest achievements on the way we hope to achieve in the next 20 years. But I also think that if Google was the only thing we create, I do not get too disappointed. " Page thinks otherwise: "I was very disappointed because our business has just started."

Brin explained: "We run Google a bit like running a university. We have so many projects, over 100 children. We do a lot of different areas. The only way to lead you to success is to first suffer defeat. " The crowd applauded students enthusiastic response. The idea will finally taste success after failure and mental fear of failure, students are immediately supported.

Another student asked about the new project from Google. Brin said, joking manner: "We feel embarrassed when talking about our new project. There is an Israeli. Yossi (Vardi, who invented instant messaging) has a friend who produced his underwear, Calvin Klein underwear company.

So we're trying to see if we can work together to make a slip signal is not Google. " He asked: "If Google underwear manufacturer, who will buy it?". The arms raised. Brin to add: "It is one of the few projects related to technical matters most that we're doing."

From this arises another question immediately: So Google make money from? Page replied: "Every search result, more or less, are required to pay Google, mainly through advertising. People pay for advertising. We are fortunate to have chosen the type related to ads instead of banner ads to run. This helps us get the best search engine. We make a profit by paying other companies, such as AOL, by using our search engine. "

Another student asked about competition from Google. Page replied: "Start, Google has to compete with Excite, Alta Vista and other sites. These sites not only focus on each search engine, so we do not have many problems arise as they do. Today, we face many more challenges and competition.

We have over 1,000 employees working at Google. We are preparing to open offices worldwide. It is part of why we travel around the world. This is a real test for us. The most difficult is that we can achieve this in the long term, become a company with 10-20 years of age, or we will be annexed. "
Page added: "The invention of something and have a big

idea is a big workload. But that's not enough. You have to let the whole world to know it. At Google, we combine the capabilities of science, mathematics, computer skills and get people to work hard. "

That year, Page and Brin was only 30 years old!

Google Company

Larry Page met Sergey Brin in the spring of 1995. Although few months younger than Page, but Brin learned at Stanford University for two years. Brin graduated from college at age 19, ten outstanding pass tests required to enroll in Ph.D. at Stanford University was the first test, and easily join the team and the professors.

Page met Brin

Both Larry Page and Sergey Brin were born into a family tradition of hospitality and intellectuals, especially in the areas of computer science, mathematics and future study. Page was born on 26-3-1973 in the U.S., Page's mother is Jewish, also announced his cult of technology. Brin was born on 21-8-1973, his parents left the Soviet

Brin's parents are also the rich knowledge of science and technology. His mother was a full scientific achievements at Goddard Space Center of NASA. Page and Brin focused on pursuing doctoral degrees, not to get rich.

Their families, nothing is more prestigious higher education. In addition to pride in the way that their parents' intellectual pursuits, both hope to become Stanford University's doctoral someday. Both barely think that your educational experience here then they have chosen will be tested.

May 1-1996, Page and Brin with the students and faculty at Stanford University computer science to a new place: a beautiful four-storey building beige stone engraved with William Gates Department of Informatics. Chairman of Microsoft - Bill Gates - have contributed $ 6 million for construction of buildings, with the money that Bill Gates has the right to name the building. Page 360 Gates in the room along with four other students. Brin was assigned to a different office, but he still spent more time working with Page in Gates room 360.

Gates Room 360 looks like a small forest, with trees to climb on the ceiling extractor pinch. In one corner, under the table of Page, they placed a computer model from Lego pieces. Both never thought that one day they will compete with the giant Bill Gates.

Page One of the topics discussed like it was invented system of data mining priority over Vietnam. They formed a new team called MIDAS, which stands for Data Mining at Stanford phrase (data mining, Stanford University). In Greek legend, King Midas is a magic ability: impact on something, that turned into gold.

While data mining, they do experiments conveniently arranged so that information on the Internet is developing a strong organization but messy. In the mid-1990s, millions of visitors and start communicating via email, but researchers began seriously annoyed the middle of a "forest" site. Meanwhile, the Ph.D. students at Stanford University, Jerry Yang and David Filo, was looking for another method. Do not just rely on each technology, they hired a team of editors sitting selected sites in order of the alphabet. They named their company is Yahoo.

Although their method has simplified the search only valuable information, but it is not comprehensive and do not keep up rushing the development of the site Brin also have tried the tools and contacts, but no other search site optimized at all. Brin increasingly convinced that there must be a better way to search for information online. Meanwhile, Page - an ambitious - to download the entire worldwide web to your computer.

A check for $ 100,000

Page heard of the idea may seem silly rather than daring.

He even announced that downloads the entire site down fairly easily and quickly. However, Page very seriously and embarked on the task of implementing his ideas. Brin and Page believe that have found the subject for their dissertation.

In early 1997, Page has created the basic search tools, he named this tool is BackRub because it links to related sites, helping users sort search results by an order logic. First is a search on the Internet to reach useful results quickly.

The fall of 1997, Brin and Page decided to replace BackRub a different name. Page found a name that no one had ever eye-catching set is hard. Therefore, he asked his roommate Sean Anderson helped his research.

Anderson recalls, "I wrote my ideas on the table but he would not fit. Takes several days so he began discouraging and we continue to think together. I sat beside the table and one of the last idea is: why does not the Googleplex it?

My suggestion: When did you set up a company to search and look up, to help people organize the mountain of data. Googleplex means that a huge number. He liked the name. He said: So why are we not try Google? He wants more concise. I type in Google, misspelled words and no one has registered the name. Page found or, after that he registered the name at that night and wrote on the blackboard Google.com. The next morning I went to the office, it adds up Tamara wrote: You spelled wrong. It must be a googol. Of course, everything was arranged. "

In 1997, the search engine will only be widely disseminated throughout Stanford, everyone mouth are about Google. Because the database and number of users increases, Brin and Page needed more computers. Lack of money, they save by buying parts and assembling itself took, then they unload the port, "borrowing" the computer derelict. The instructor, who say they are very needy, they donated $ 10,000 amount from an electronic library project at Stanford. After collecting so many computers to office Gates 360 filled, they turn the bedroom into Page's data centers.

On a sunny day in California last month 8-1998, Page and Brin sitting porch to a house in Palo Alto eagerly waiting for "angel of Silicon Valley" is Andy Bechtolsheim, a well-known investors. After Page and Brin tested and presented the talk, Bechtolsheim appreciate and understand the breakthrough by which Google can bring great results.

Immediately, he offered to give them a check to buy a computer and he can continue to discuss with them further in the following meetings. No further negotiations, Bechtolsheim wrote a check for $ 100,000 subject to "Google the company."

Porsche Bechtolsheim going reporters that morning, not knowing the great importance he has done. He then confided: "In my thinking, they would have been millions of people use Google and they will pick the money."

When Brin and Page left Stanford University the fall of 1998, pursuing the construction of the best search engine in the world, they moved the machine, equipment and toys into their garage and some room in the a house with hot tub near Menlo Park. Brin and Page hired an area that can cost $ 1,500 per month but they have chosen to pay $ 1,700 per month to not have to pay additional fees and taxes any more and everything cool down the roof in the first row.

Dated 7-9-1998, they formally established company Google. Then they opened the first bank account and sent a check for $ 100,000 worth of Bechtolsheim on it. They hire Craig Silverstein, the subject attended Stanford University PhD, as its first employee.

Google: Conquering the markets
There are times Google seemed unable to keep up with demand, which is when Sergey Brin and Larry Page have spent $ 1 million amount originally invested.

After only five months, the garage was not enough room for the machinery of Brin and Page. Therefore, beginning in 1999, they moved his office to University Avenue in Palo Alto, Stanford University is just one mile.

The shirt was too tight.

Shortly after moving to new offices in Palo Alto, Google already has eight employees are working hard to keep up with increased search requests per day. Throughout the years, the number of searches per day to more than 500,000 visitors, the PC Magazine site top 100 ranking and top search engine in 1998. The shirt was too tight, it is clear that Brin and Page needs more money to purchase additional computer systems, but both these guys do not want to lose control of his company.

In an environment of strong growth in Silicon Valley in 1999, attracting capital through listing on stock market prices is an easy way for Google even though these companies do not make a profit.

But if the market listing, Brin and Page did not want to disclose trade secrets and methods of its own, attracting more investors are no longer generous feasible, because the money they need now is large. They began licensing companies to use its search technology on the internal network or external network. They find it difficult to convince people to pay for services when people are looking for that finding was not significant. They need money from outside sources. "Any situation which has the solution" - they say.

Page and Brin have to learn to resolve financial problems. They decided to attract investments through a finance company without losing control of the company. Thanks to the advice of knowledgeable investors in technology such as Jeff Bezos, Amazon.com chief, Brin and Page decided to cooperate with two of the financial investment company names and most prestigious Silicon Valley: Kleiner Perkins and Sequoia Capital.

In this era of booming online companies, including John Doerr - Kleiner Perkins and Director Michael Moritz - Sequoia Capital's directors are tired of each other to listen to lengthy presentations by PowerPoint on new business ideas. For the two giant investment firms in the financial sector in Silicon Valley, Brin and Page as a new atmosphere. Moritz and Sequoia Capital Financial Corporation has invested his $ 2 million in Yahoo and reap $ 32 million back from the launch of Yahoo's IPO in 1996.

In 1999, Google began a lack of money to invest. One of a kind to investors, a financial manager in Silicon Valley named Ron Conway Moritz contacted and asked him to arrange an appointment to meet with Brin and Page. Moritz said: "Ron Conway recalled that I remembered them. I've also been known to them by the people at Yahoo. Islam is the spring of 1999, so everything was prepared very quickly. At that point, everything is urgent. "

Can not be "swallowed alive fresh"

Days passed, the two boys realize why the venture was nicknamed investors "fresh life to swallow," and they think it is better has nothing to both the this investment.

Brin and Page asked if Conway can arrange a group of investors to replace the two benefactors of this investment. Attracted a group of passive investors means that Brin and Page will still hold control of the company. Conway said they told that they plan to do, adding that time is also an important factor because they are gradually running out of money for

investment.

However, instead of contacting investor philanthropist, Conway decided to Moritz and Doerr said that if they did not find any way to start cooperation and the Google guys and they'll have to get yourself very seriously in this work.
Although at that time, both firms Kleiner Perkins and Sequoia have stopped investing in a lot of businesses to invest in companies operating in the newly established network, bells rang in their heads: there is something it is

extremely hidden potential in the pair. Just a few days, Conway and Shriram have convinced them. Kleiner Perkins and Sequoia Capital, each party will invest $ 12.5 million in Google, for a total amount of investment is 25 million and each side contributing half, and both agree with Brin and Page's request that they remain The main control.

However, by their very large investment into a Google account so, Doerr and Moritz has added a condition to be used that amount of investment: they have pledged to hire an experienced manager to help them This search tool into a real money machine.

This is a very reasonable demands by the fact that companies do not have Google as a business plan anything specific. Thus, Brin and Page are willing to agree, provided they have the money to invest $ 25 million and have control of the company, they will facilitate consensus and to hire someone as CEO Released for business smoothly. But there it is: they do not intend to hire someone, then they must report to work with him.

Dated 7-6-1999, less than a year after they leave Stanford, Brin and Page put out a press release, the two companies announced financial Kleiner Perkins and Sequoia Capital have agreed to invest $ 25 million in Google , Doerr and Moritz joined the board of Google. Two boys, who are more confident students in class, there is a huge amount of money that does not seem to lose anything in return. This demonstrates that the two Google guys had a perfect deal: they get money to build the search engine they desire, just keep control of the company.

Autumn of 1999, Google started adding equipment repair shop, Google has expanded from 300 units to 2,000 units on the computer after just one month, and in the summer of next year that number has doubled. Google has two data centers in northern California and a district center Tuesday in Washington DC, then open a lot more centers across the U.S. and the world.

Google - Shaking hands, "Mr. Big"

Stock market of the Internet provider declined severely in 2000. Losing, bankruptcy occurs everywhere in Silicon Valley but did not happen with Google.

This period is "not better" for the development of strong and firm Google. Software engineers and mathematicians names, who suddenly realized he had been unemployed or holding a stock pile like a bunch of paper roll, the chances are not two of them are devoted

"Do not be a devil"

When you are on the rise, the main competitor of Google, at which Microsoft is facing huge obstacles. January 6000-2000, Microsoft has opened a major case controversial. During the lawsuit, Bill Gates - Microsoft boss, is also the lawsuits - which many described as bullying or who take a proprietary name.

By the end of the case, when the Supreme Court judge Thomas Penfield Jackson federally declared the constraints of the Internet Explorer browser in Windows operating system violated antitrust, Microsoft has a bitter losing money millions dollars. Once again, Google again benefit from the event and time.

Many engineers worked with Microsoft realized that it's like a lord in the field of software, whereas Google is a business feel fresh with shining halo around the high beds slogan " Do not be a devil "and proudly with the two young founders are known as the two handsome guys.

The love of the growing use of Google Google has created motivation to go further. This company was rated as the leading company in the field of Internet search users, with 99% confirmed the superiority Vietnam compared to competitors. Google is also paying attention to market the university, give them the familiar colorful logo and search box on their site, nurturing new talent

The New Yorker magazine of the month 5-2000 has described Google as a search engine for the majority. " Also this month, The Times Digital has praised Google as saying that "Google as laser sharp, while the competition only as a blunt sword."

As other technology companies in Silicon Valley is preparing to close, Sergey Brin and Larry Page unfurl banners down the street: "Do not be discouraged. Google will soon come to the French, German, Italian, Swedish, Finnish, Spanish, Portuguese, Dutch, Norwegian and Danish. "

Google homepage has been translated into several different languages to promote the internationalization process by its more convenient features. Google also began to introduce wireless search features, so that users can use Google's services by mobile phone.

Then, instead of waiting for users to come to Google.com, the company began actively promoting business activities and promote their brands. In oogle's new program, the website news, sales and other site can register to place a Google search box on their homepage, it just gives customers the ability to use Google has money from the intermediary service.

Deal Yahoo, AOL began.

Months of 6000-2000, Google made a big step towards global recognition with the signing of an agreement with Internet provider Yahoo parallel to provide the search results generated from Google.

This acquisition has expanded its presence and image of Google on the web, bringing it to millions of other users every day. Brin evaluate the agreement with Yahoo "is a milestone for Google and a strong evidence for Google's business strategy." In early 2001, Google does something else amazing, it was allowed to perform 100 million searches per day and 10,000 permits searches per second. Google also entered the American dictionary as a verb.

When the terrorist attacks on the United States occurred on 11-9-2001, Google's search traffic has overloaded. "A series of major news sites are overloaded due to too large flow capacity and can not transmit the information to be hot - Brin and Page have been recorded - Google has done its utmost to meet demand by offering versions of stories archive news on Google's home page and continue to fully convey the important information around the world.

During weekdays or in special events like this, Google - with 66 different languages - are gradually woven into the texture of American culture, while the structure of the world community.

These figures show that last year the business strategy

of Page and Brin are succeeding. A company with only three years old had a much better position than other companies in the Internet field.

The constant focus on innovation and developing appropriate corporate culture has created momentum for the introduction of new products and areas for development and business sectors. Traffic is growing constantly. And the ads have started bringing revenue, although things are just beginning, Google receives an annual profit since its first ad about 7 million.

In 2002, Google reached new heights finance. 1-5 days, the company America Online (AOL) web property in connection with 34 million Internet subscribers got Google as the search engine of choice on his website. Starting from this point on all site users of the AOL service has a small search box with the contents of "Google Search". The scale of AOL has expanded the scope of Google more than any other Google partners that can work together during that time. This result is a competitive job because Google has beat rival advertising company is looking Overtune previously provided ads for AOL to work with AOL.

The Google link with AOL as AOL back again against Microsoft. For years, Microsoft often threatened to remove AOL's services by investing more money to promote Internet services is capable of competing with MSN and they are providing free e-mail through the

After the company finished buying Netscape, AOL can only be wiped out when Microsoft provide free Internet Explorer browser for Internet users. AOL filed a lawsuit at this Microsoft because the action is unfair and does not cause competitive harm to AOL.

For its part, Microsoft Corporation Overtune chosen to provide ads for its search service. During the war when the public as confidential between Google and Microsoft, both parties want to do its utmost to gain the upper hand, gain competitive advantage.

5 myths about Microsoft

There is a symbol of Bill Gates can explain the common interest for our business and the legendary creation of his most famous, Microsoft Corporation.
Photo shows a 19-year-old men with glasses smug smile and familiar approach. We wonder how a student that looks silly problems driving skills (and wearing a shirt on the flowers) could become the world's richest people?
If you go to find answers online, you will find a lot of false information. That does not help Microsoft make up more

than half the market than its competitors in recent years. It does not help as the competitors have a place to share their envy of the world. They have accused the company and former executives on the implementation mode exclusive to seize the biggest technological advances and becomes really evil.

The stories of damage around Microsoft and its founder has close ties with the advent of personal computers. To start a list of 5 myths about Microsoft, we will explore a misunderstanding about the origin of "windows"

1: Bill Gates is the devil.

Arrogant. Bullying. Cruel. Stubborn. These are all from that colleague and former competitor and now Microsoft has used to describe William Henry Gates III. But critics describe him as a cruel person? Never.

Gates announced that he will stop managing the daily operations at Microsoft in July 2008. Some compared to Henry Ford, who had taken a technological rare, expensive and tricky to figure out how to sell to the public.

Microsoft's long-term task is "desktop in every home." Indeed, were present on the Windows PC 1.75 billion worldwide in 1981.

Some journalists and experts have been selected to compare Gates voiHenry Ford, but a more appropriate comparison might be Andrew Carnegie, the steel giant to engage in a ruthless business before dedicating the last years of his life to philanthropy. When he died in 1919, he wanted to give all his possessions to museums, libraries, parks and other charities.

Gates may have more crime because of illegal business tactics, but a philanthropist. He was ready to become the largest contribution in the history of the world. Charitable Bill and Melinda Gates Foundation has invested tens of billions of dollars to remove disease and poverty in developing countries and will eventually give all the wealth of the Gates. Such stars may be considered cruel?

2: Microsoft is not innovative.

Microsoft has a reputation in the world worthy of attracting software technology. In other words, Microsoft has borrowed or purchased every good idea that it ever had.

This theory is not unfounded. For example, Bill Gates and friends do not write code for MS-DOS. They bought QDOS (Quick and Dirty Operating System) with $ 50,000, tweak it and licensing for IBM for huge profits. They are not Internet Explorer code base. They licensed the source code from Spyglass Inc., maker of the Mosaic browser, and use the same code base for three or four versions of Explorer.

Protection for those companies that Microsoft is not a great technological innovation - Gates did not realize the potential of the Internet until 1995 - but they will say that the company had some ideas business the most advanced in this field.

Think about it. Before Microsoft appears, no one has the idea of selling software and hardware together. IBM received licensing of Microsoft MS-DOS because it wanted to focus on hardware. Gates, Steve Ballmer and other Microsoft executives first looked to be potentially profitable to license its operating system for tens of manufacturers of different computer hardware.

Harvard Institute for Business Research secret of the success of Microsoft, they correctly identify innovative approaches of the company is its intellectual property. Microsoft has created a huge library of proprietary source code that works on the Windows platform. If a developer to prove his loyalty to Microsoft, he gets access to library code - and hundreds of millions of potential customers of Microsoft.

3: Microsoft is a "natural monopoly".

Some critics of the antitrust case U.S. government against Microsoft to protect Microsoft because they think it is a natural monopoly because of their dominance by doing better than competitors on the free market.

Real definition of a natural monopoly is quite different from its usual meaning. In economic parlance, a natural monopoly is a monopoly allowed the company an industry because it is the best interests of the state and consumers.

The public service companies are examples of natural monopolies. In most cities and towns, you do not have a choice of electric companies to use. That's because there is a huge barrier to start forming the power company. You have to build power plants and power cables to create an infrastructure to each family. Would be more economical for consumers - and more effective for the state - if there is a private company to closely manage care of this.

Ostensibly, Microsoft looks like a natural monopoly of the computer industry. Because they account for 90% global market for operating systems, Microsoft is entitled to benefit from economies of scale. For example, the small software developer can never spend as much as Microsoft in product development and marketing. They'll never get back the money without having to cost more than Microsoft had paid for similar products.

The biggest difference is that Microsoft used "extraordinary power of the market and huge profits," said U.S. District Judge Thomas Penfield Jackson, to not only build higher barriers for competitors of it, but also to intimidate anyone who dared to compete with. And there is no "natural" about it

4: Microsoft does not care about security.

Microsoft is a giant among software manufacturers, is the continuous security vulnerabilities in operating systems and application software. The flaw allows hackers to access computers are not protected, move them into programs that spread malicious viruses and worms even more.

You rarely see a headline, "Apple warned users about serious security vulnerabilities" or "running Red Hat released patches to prevent hackers." That's because there are very few programmers to write malicious code and computer viruses for Mac and Linux computers. The reason is simple: If you are a hacker covertly and your goal is to harm as many machines as possible, you'll do them on the operating system used by more than 90% of

Despite criticism about the security weaknesses of Windows XP, it is wrong to say that Microsoft does not care about security. Microsoft used some characters have the sharpest minds in the field of network security, including Chairman Michael Howard and Linux security expert Crispin Cowan. In recent years, they made a number of long-term security initiative, an extensive, including Trustworthy Computing, End to End Trust and most recently, Microsoft Security Essentials. Microsoft makes Windows more secure than XP 7.

Real question, according to Rob Enderle of technology experts, is whether anyone in any company can successfully repel the attacks which are continuously imposed on Microsoft products. To make matters worse, he said, boasting about the security features will surely attract the operation mode of the hackers. For example, a message from Oracle that calls its latest creation is "bulletproof." It has been successfully attacked the next day.

5: Microsoft invented the "Windows".

In 1968, when 13 years old, Bill Gates still is learning BASIC programming atrophy, an engineer named Douglas Englebart at Stanford Research Institute introduced the mouse to the world. With modern computer users, the mouse is a need for technology: How else can you click on the icon, scroll through the menus and make the cursor move? But computer users in 1968 had found a network of mice, because no one heard about it later.

Englebart who invented the graphical user interface, or GUI (pronounced gooey - Graphics User Interface). In the early 1970s, a group of researchers at Xerox Palo Alto Research Center (PARC) to expand the concept of Englebart and manufacturing of Xerox Alto, the first personal computer but it is characteristic of the current standard " WIMP "GUI: Windows, Icons, Menus and Pointing Device.
Run on a Xerox Alto operating system environment called Smalltalk was developed to create Xerox PARC. 1979, 24 years old, Steve Jobs of Apple Computer, Inc. Apple shares to pay $ 1,000,000 for a detailed tour of Xerox PARC to see the facilities. Were impressed by the Smalltalk GUI, Jobs asked to see documentation of the product, Xerox was awarded a silly way.

With technology in the hands of the Smalltalk GUI, Apple released the Lisa in 1983, the first commercial computer with Windows GUI features. Jobs using an interface similar to the Macintosh system. When Bill Gates, who wrote the software for the Mac, released Windows 2.0 in 1987, Apple sued Microsoft for stealing blatantly appearance and feel of the Mac - something that Apple

Apple eventually lost the case and the dominance of Microsoft on the PC market as synonymous for "windows" for Windows.

Konosuke Matsushita (I): Getting started

Konosuke Matsushita was born on 27/11/1894 in a small village south of Osaka. His father was a small land lord and prestige in the community. The youngest of eight siblings, Konosuke have a pleasant childhood. However, the assets of the family Konosuke dashed when his father failed to commodity speculation and the family forced to live in a small house in the city.

Konosuke Matsushita was born on 27/11/1894 in a small village south of Osaka. His father was a small land lord and prestige in the community. The youngest of eight siblings, Konosuke have a pleasant childhood. However, the assets of the family Konosuke dashed when his father failed to commodity speculation and the family forced to live in a small house in the city.

To help families, Konosuke application for vocational training and women's sales job at a coal furnace in Osaka a few months before completing primary school. At age nine, Konosuke mother goodbye at the station, and I began a long journey to the city.

Apprentice in Osaka: 9 years

Konosuke working days of starting work at dawn to clean

the shop clean. When the store has a decent computer, he began to beat the charcoal fertilizer, while the sons of the store until then still sleeping in bed drunk.

However, ultimately, on the first field is to pay, and 5 cents (sen) he only seems to be getting a fortune and really tired all disappear.

Less than a year, coal stores closed. Konosuke would be on the side job at a bike shop, at the time, is a luxury item imported from England. Bike shops also carry all the small mechanical repairs, and Konosuke quickly learned to use lathes and other tools.

Be treated as a family member shop owner, has 5 years Konosuke happy here.

Konosuke have sometimes wanted to quit his job at the bike shop to find another job that allows him to complete the study at evening classes, but his father persuaded him to stay Konosuke. He said "The children are learning skills will ensure your child's future. Be a successful entrepreneur and you can hire people who are fully educated. "

At this time, electric cars began to appear on the big square in Osaka, Konosuke instincts told that the use of energy products will create a new wave of the future. Anxious to become a part of this new field, you would like to work at Electric Lighting Co., Osaka, and leave the bike shop at age 15.

The first major project that is getting involved Konosuke wiring for the city's major theaters. The project lasted more than six months and Konosuke team worked day and night to catch up. Although the project successful,

Konosuke had pneumonia due to long time working in theater with no heating system.

Marriages arranged by families are very popular in Japan at that time, spring 1915, Konosuke sister introduced her to his friends of his, Mumeno. Several months later, the couple's wedding was held and the walls bear the responsibility of Konosuke a new family.

Established companies and start trading power socket: 1917, 22

Konosuke career continues to grow at the Osaka Electric Light Company. He was soon asked to take the higher paying position. 22 years old, he became a supervisor, the highest position a technician can dream.

Before that, Konosuke was unsuccessful in persuading a person in charge of applying measures to improve the electrical outlet by his own design and manufacture test in your spare time. With the new job, Konosuke have much time to think about than the socket.

Still remember his father's advice about the advantages of an entrepreneur, he left a stable job with high salaries on 15/06/1917 and opened their own production company. The entire savings of Konosuke less than 100 yen at that time, just near enough for the tools and basic materials. Heavy tools, of course, is not possible. However, not frustrated with meager resources, Konosuke open a store in the small apartment in the basement of a building by themselves. I have worked with two former colleagues at Osaka and electricity companies of Mumeno youngest brother, Toshio. Business was very bad electrical outlet, and the end of 1917, two former colleagues Konosuke leave.

Companies are left with only three people: Konosuke, and Toshio Mumeno.

The owner of the pawn shop Mumeno story about the long months of shock and shoulders bear, meal of meals for each family. Is on the verge of bankruptcy, the company has completely saved any orders by a 1000 piece of insulation for electric fans.

Starting business: 23, 1918

When the business started to grow, Konosuke have money to invest. He rented a two-story house and open shop electrical Matsushita made on the first floor.

Have a larger workshop, Konosuke expand production further development of plug and socket connector socket on both ends .. Both are innovative ideas from his own design.

These products are quickly used extensively, and gives the company the image quality with low price. By 1922, Konosuke to build a plant and the new office to meet expanding production needs.

Konosuke Matsushita (II): The beginning of the giant Design and sell bike lamps: 28, 1923

In 1923, Konosuke realize the enormous potential market for battery-powered lamp cycling. Although this bike lights have appeared, but generally have low reliability and use time typically no more than three consecutive hours.

Decided to solve this problem, Konosuke for six months to design lights for a bullet bike, especially, this type of bulb can operate for 40 hours without charging. However, the sales agent did not put much faith in this product and refused to supply the market.

Konosuke decided to bypass the agent and send samples directly to the bike shop owner, suggested they check the results of the operation of new light bulbs. The move brings the decision result is a flood of orders. The former agent did not even talk to Konosuke sad, now, by contrast, are competing to distribute new products.

Using the first National brand: 32, 1927

Konosuke continue developing the next generation battery-powered bicycle lamp second with a square design. While thought to name the new bulbs, I suddenly saw English words "international" on the report.

Look in the dictionary, Konosuke understand that inside the word "international" from "national" means "belonging or relating to people of a nation." This meaning of the perfect new product. Konosuke believe that there will be a day when all families throughout Japan will use it. So in 1927, the National brand was born.

Introduce "super-irons": 32, 1927

At this time, the electrical products are considered luxury goods and the price is too high for most consumers.

Konosuke decided to create electrical products in line with the solvency of the consumer population. He set up separate departments specializing in the design of the electric heater and electric irons with development aimed at large market.

Three months later, "Super discuss the" National brand was developed. Although the table is market power demand forecast is 100,000 a year, Konosuke has asked the production department is to provide effective National Desk Super 10,000 monthly. He said that large-scale production will help reduce costs, and many consumers will buy new tables as soon as the price is consistent with their solvency. Thus, the market will expand. National Desk is super effective to sell for 3.2 yen, much lower rates of 5 yen competitors and quickly become a more product-selling company.

Began producing radio: 36, 1931

During recessions, demand for rapid development of radio people. However, the price is too high radio and low quality products. But there Konosuke radio products in the model are three tubes in three months. This product immediately received the first prize in the contest by Radio Tokyo public institutions.

To accelerate the growth of new media, Konosuke acquired patent rights to use two important manufacturing and public radio.

Announcing the company's mission in meeting the

Konosuke be a friend invited to attend a ceremony at the Shinto shrine. He was very impressed with mutually supporting roles of religion and business, "Human beings need both material prosperity and spiritual. Religion lead people to overcome difficulties with happiness and serenity. Business and contribute items essential for a happy life. This is the essential mission of the business. "

After returning, Konosuke focus employees on 05/05/1932 and message-oriented statement for the company for several decades. "The mission of a manufacturer alleviation of poverty by producing so many goods. Although water can also be seen as a product, no one will object if a passersby to stop and drink water from public taps. That's because water supplies are plentiful and cheap water rates. The mission of a manufacturer as we are providing goods and rr as many public water. That's how we get rid of poverty, bring happiness to human life, and make the world a better place. " Deployment management system independent (Autonomous system-Divisional management system): 38, 1933

Konosuke division and held a management system independently. The company is divided into three parts: (i) radio production, (ii) manufacturing dry batteries and lighting devices, and (iii) production of power systems, plastics and other man-made electric heater . Each department has its own administrative activities and self-responsible production. Thereby, Konosuke may assign more responsibility to managers, while also giving them the opportunity to learn every aspect of business-from product development to sales.

Plant and the construction of a new office in Kadoma, Osaka 38, 1933

The company is now producing over 200 products and Konosuke noticed the time was to expand the scale. May 07/1933 the company moved to the new office and factory at Kadoma, Osaka southeast.

Institute for establishment of human resource training: 39, 1934

Konosuke's favorite saying: Business is human (Business is people). Always believe in the capacity of staff and colleagues are part of Konosuke character. By 1934, he founded the Institute for training in Kadoma plant. Here, high school students can study for three years and is training both technical and business.

Incorporation of civil commerce Matshusita (Matsushita Electric Trading Company): 40, 1935

In 1932, Konosuke established commercial department in

charge of research and development capabilities of companies selling products on the international market. Export sales growing rapidly, Konosuke decision to raise the commercial department of Trade Company electrical

Matshushita (Matsushita Electric Trading Company) in May 8 / 1935. At that time, this is a very unusual move for a manufacturer of electrical products. However, Konosuke really believe that international markets should also be considered as the domestic market. The company will also perform commercial activities in sync with Matsushita's business philosophy.

Establishment of industrial labor union Matsushita: 51, 1946

Dated 16/08/1945, a day after Japan surrendered unconditionally, Konosuke summoned senior executives and announced plans to continue production of consumer goods. Four days later, in a speech calling for all his workers, he said: "Manufacturing is extremely important foundation for the process of our recovery. Let's wake Matsushita spiritual tradition, and the task of national reconstruction, and to improve the lives of Japanese people. "
Under the command of General MacArthur, occupation

forces quickly implement democratic reform process in Japan, including the establishment of labor unions.

Present at the ceremony in the eyes of industrial labor union Matsushita, held at the center of Nakanoshima, Osaka, Konosake immediately received support from the employees through collective message that he placed a high priority best interests of the employees and the best policies harmonizing the interests of workers and the manager will be made.

Institute for establishment PHP: 51, 1946

Japanese society after the war ravaged by inflation, food shortages and dishonest business. May 11/1946, Konosuke established organization with a primary concern is to improve living conditions. Based on the slogan "Peace, Happiness and Prosperity comes from," he named the organization the Institute of PHP (Peace and Happiness through Prosperity), and began publishing in the Journal of PHP. PHP Institute began implementing global operations since 1970.

To the U.S.: 56, 1951 ·

In the target annual management policy in 1951,

declared it was time Konosuke map of Matsushita Electric to take position in the international economic community. He warned his team to respect the cultural values and traditions by their going to turn active phase with the global scale.

Konosuke decision to the U.S. to explore their own modes of operation of industrial conglomerate United States. He noticed a huge gap between American prosperity and poverty in Japan, observed that "the first condition for prosperity is a social structure that allows each individual maximize the capacity and talent them. "

To compete with the West, he noticed that his company should have better knowledge about electricity and electrical, and need a specialized approach to higher product development.

Technical cooperation with Philips: 57, 1952

Belief that advanced western technology is the key to success for the reconstruction process in Japan, Konosuke start searching business partners abroad. In 1952, after tough negotiations, Matsushita Electric and Philips of the Netherlands has come to an agreement on technical cooperation, joint venture and Matsushita Electronics Corporation. But from the beginning, the negotiators had asked Philips enjoy a higher percentage of sales activities with technical assistance, but ruled against Konosuke Matsushita Electric point value equal contributions by experience management and requires the partners to pay a fee for management support activities. Eventually, the two sides come to a commitment to equal cooperation.

Announced expansion plans in 5 years: 61, 1956

In 1956, when the government claimed to have successfully completed the country's economic reconstruction, Konosuke surprised his team and the entire industry with the introduction of a plan to expand production scale ambitious 5 years, with annual sales quadrupled, the number of employees increased by 60%, and capital assets increased from three billion to 10 billion yen. "Success is guaranteed," he declared, "because these numbers reflected the public's desire for the men who signed the contract we are invisible." Konosuke has achieved the goals that seemed impossible after just over 4 years.

Electrification boom: late 1950

Continuous economic growth in Japan brought booming sales of electrical products and electrical equipment manufacturer first started entering the market, leading to fierce competition on product prices. The new devices appear and help of family life on a pleasant and efficient. All consumers want to own televisions, washing machines, refrigerators, also called "three sacred chalice." Konosuke forecast times are electrification and efforts to strengthen the sales network and a stable market with the establishment of the retail network inextricably linked.

Received a medal from the Queen awarded the Netherlands: 63, 1958
In June, received a medal Konosuke "Commander in the Order of Orange-Nassau" by Queen of the Netherlands awarded at a ceremony held at the Dutch Embassy in Tokyo. This is the highest accolades of the Royal Netherlands in foreign relations.

This is the award was given "by the great contribution for economic cooperation as well as developing the friendly cooperative relations between the two countries." Konosuke the first to receive this honor from the Queen of the Netherlands after World War II. He continues to contribute to cooperation between the two countries to become the founder and president of the Dutch Friendship Association in Kansai, Japan in 1959. Konosuke also received many medals from other countries for his contributions in developing cooperation with Japan as Medalie Merito De Honra Ao Cultural Award of the Brazilian government in April 1968, Commandeur de L'Ordre de la Couronne King Award from Belgium September 10/1972, and Panglima Mangku Negara and the title of King of Malaysia Tan Sri from 2 / 1979.

Matsushita Electric Corporation founded in America: 64, 1959

In 1959, ready to expand business activities abroad, Konosuke established the first trading company Matsushita Electric Corporation in New York. He urged his managers to quickly adapt to local environment and efforts to make products for American consumers appreciate. Also during this time, he built many factories in countries like Thailand (1961) and Taiwan (1962). Konosuke Matsushita (end) - Dreams Unlimited

Leave the operating position and the president: 65, 1961

At the meeting the annual management policy for 1961, there Konosuke speech announced the company achieved its target of 5-year plan and is entering a new period of growth. Ending his speech, he was astounded when the entire audience left the position statement the

Director General. "I just celebrated the 65th birthday. I always thought I should stop at a suitable time and that time has come. I will always support the company as chairman but no longer participate in the daily operating activities. "
Appeared on the cover of TIME and LIFE magazines: 67, 1962

The statements and comments Konosuke on mass media is widely respected Japanese people. When the success of Matsushita Electric began to spread abroad, as well as Konosuke Matsushita is seen as one of the greatest entrepreneurs the world. Series of important international figures visiting companies, including U.S. Attorney General Robert Kennedy, Indian Prime Minister Indira Gandhi, and President of Yugoslavia (former) Tito. Konosuke themselves always lead the guests to visit companies and individuals together to exchange ideas.

Foreign press quickly towards the interest on Matsushita Electric and its founder. February, 1962 appearing on the cover Konosuke TIME magazine, weekly news magazines popular in the U.S.. In 1963, Matsushita Konosuke and Mumeno attend the "party of the century", on the occasion of 40th anniversary by Time magazine in New York.

9 / 1964, Konosuke appear in LIFE magazine and was described as an "industry leading", "who made the most money", "philosopher", "magazine publisher", and " author of best-selling works. " Fin press took Konosuke

Matsushita and Matsushita Electric to become prominent worldwide.
Invited the president of sales and distribution of Matsushita to attend a conference for 3 days: 69, 1964

Matsushita's profits for the first time since a serious fall in 1950 due to economic growth of Japan's hot start slowed and fluctuate and fall into recession To cope with the difficult situation, Konosuke Matsushita to invite the president of the company's dealer sales and Matsushita to three-day conference at the hot springs of Atami, south of Tokyo .

Sales companies and distributors blame Matsushita on its economic difficulties. However, the manager of Matsushita says that the capacity of poor management of the sales companies and distributors is the problem.

Mark Zuckerberg, Facebook founder

At age 25, Mark Zuckerberg has in hand $ 1 billion and is the youngest billionaire appeared in the list of Forbes 400 billionaires. Mark Zuckerberg is also the founder and chief executive officer (CEO) of the Facebook social networking.

Born in 1984 in a Jewish-American family whose father is a dentist and mother is a psychologist, he was Mark Zuckerberg have a passion for technology intense. This has included "golden boys" in the information technology industry to succeed today.

From the initial test

Mark Zuckerberg began programming computers when he was still a secondary student. Mark at that boy is really interested in the development and upgrading of computer programs, especially the online communication tools and games (game).

When she walked into Phillips Exeter Schools, Mark has developed a computer application programs such as programs to help workers who worked in his father's office to communicate with each other, the game "Risk" Synapse and program music. The initial creation of the Mark has been the attention of information technology in the U.S. at that time, including Microsoft and America Online (AOL).

Both large corporations are trying to convince to buy the copyright program Synapse and Mark want to work for him, but Mark decided to study at Harvard University.

By 2002, Mark began entering the auditorium of Harvard University, a prestigious university top American. Here, he has done many projects on your favorite technology. Mark Coursematch project implementation to allow students to participate can view a list of other students enrolled with their general subject. This project was pretty much in response to students.

Dated 02/04/2004, just two years later, Mark released by Facebook that assessment at the time Mark was a project to commemorate this time in school called "Harvard-Thing." Actually, this idea is derived from Mark since he learned in high school Phillips Exeter, the program allows visitors can learn about the students, majors, faculty ...

After only four hours, with 450 hits and the school immediately sever the Internet connection of Mark, and chided him on charges of security violations of school computer networks, stealing information to post on its website. Acknowledge the error and do not be discouraged, Mark continued to upgrade research and Facebook on the principle of information available to the consent of the individual or organization and the next project.

Mark Zuckerberg admitted the owner of Microsoft billionaire Bill Gates is the inspiration that he left Harvard School's reputation to make his dream. It all started when in 2004, Bill Gates to Harvard to speak with students. At that time, Bill Gates has encouraged students to make projects that they desire, even suspend the school to pursue his dream as he did. So Mark and fellow Harvard undergraduate Moskovitz decided to leave Silicon Valley, California to wholeheartedly for Facebook.

To success with Facebook

Mark Zuckerberg moved to Palo Alto, California with Moskovitz and a few other friends. They rented a small house and office life. In summer 2004, Mark met Peter Thiel who invested in the company of Mark. So you also have offices in both the first proper summer this year.

Mark had said, during this difficult period, the group intends to return to Harvard in the fall of that year but eventually the team was in California. And until now, he has not returned to school to finish degree programs. Facebook growing rapidly. Number of members to about 60 million people and is expected to number 70 million by year's end. Facebook is the site of a digital image in the U.S. with over 8.5 million photos are uploaded each day.

Yes this is thanks to you Mark Zuckerberg and his team continually upgraded to facilitate Facebook users. Dated 5/6/2006, Facebook launched News Feed tool allows visitors to recognize your friends are doing on this site.

To Date 5/24/2007, Mark said on Facebook Platform, a foundation program for developing social applications, including Facebook social network connections. This statement actually has created excitement and interest for the group of Mark.

Within weeks, a series of applications have been built and some of them already have millions of users. So far, more than 400,000 people knowledgeable about writing computer programs worldwide to participate in building applications for Facebook Platform.

Only a month later, on 06/11/2007, Mark published on social advertising system in Los Angeles. Part of the Facebook Beacon program will allow people to share information with a network of friends on Facebook through the activities on other websites. For example, a trader selling on eBay can also be groups of friends on Facebook know this work through News Feed.
On 23/07/2008, Mark continued to announce Facebook Connect, a version of Facebook Platform in building social applications on other websites.
Before the development of Facebook dizziness, some giants in the information technology industry, including Yahoo, Viacom has sought to negotiate acquisition of this company. In 2006, Yahoo Chief Executive Terry Semel has a reputation to buy Facebook for $ 1 billion, but Mark Zuckerberg and his team did not seemed to care.

That number becomes small when on 24/10/2007, Microsoft spent $ 240 million to buy back 1.6% stake in Facebook. Zuckerberg and Facebook all employees must have gratitude for such a Bill Gates, Facebook's market value up to $ 15 billion by many experts as the actual market value of Facebook Inc. (the Company's founder Mark) lower more.

In the role of executive director and CEO of Facebook, Zuckerberg owns 20% stock and in theory, if the shares sold off its 23-year-old guy have in hand $ 3 billion.

Facebook's value to increase the number of users to freeze up every day, which some experts say, the property of not only young Zuckerberg 3 billion that could reach $ 5 billion depending on the success Facebook's coming out of the building ad networks.

Also this year, Mark Zuckerberg honor awarded Best Startup CEO of Crunchie Award 2007.

Desire to return to Harvard.

5 years ago, when wet foot dry foot to California, Mark set up business with two empty hands: no money, no house, no car ... Now that has become the CEO of Facebook Inc., he still wears jeans, and Adidas sandals to life quite confidential.

In a press conference on investment by Microsoft, Mark Zuckerberg is not even attend that to work again for the other executive officer of Facebook. This is understandable because in an interview with Forbes magazine, Mark confesses that he is not interested in whether you become a CEO or management company or not but what I really care that are do what you love and create something really appealing.

Mark still lives in a room that rent furniture is simple and every day he is riding a bike or walk to the Facebook headquarters near his apartment.
Much success but of course Mark Zuckerberg is starting to face many challenges. Some of Mark's classmates at Harvard (now operating as opposed ConnectU website) has filed a lawsuit he plagiarized website set up social connections to help them set up a project in 2003.

The plaintiff - the founders of rival site ConnectU - forced Zuckerberg criminal copyright infringement, fraud and stealing trade secrets, and to close Facebook. Facebook counterattack by ConnectU have accused the illegal entry into databases to steal thousands of e-mail address in the example of efforts to use Facebook to Connectu.

Besides the lawsuit, Mark Zuckerberg is expected to face pressure after the Microsoft investment. This is pretty easy to understand by the participation of corporate giants, Facebook's partners will have more difficult "way" to gain more benefits in the collaboration. Moreover, the advertising contract on Facebook seems certain is limited.

Success or failure is Mark Zuckerberg also pleased with the experience and achievements gained in his past few years. There are no official statistics but many analysts

This guy is compared with Microsoft Chairman Bill Gates and CEO Steve Jobs of Apple. He has come a long way and sometimes he wanted to retire. Mark Zuckerberg said he would consider returning to Harvard to complete college program.

Pierre Omidyar - Founder of Ebay: Want to succeed there must be passion

Omidyar was born on 21/61/1967 in Paris, in a family of Iranian immigrants. Omidyar was six years old, his family moved to Washington DC to his father - a physicist could pursue work in the Medical Center of John Hopkins University. Omidyar's parents divorced when he was just two years old and although Omidyar lives with his mother but his father had great influence in the life of Omidyar later. Major study in the years of Andrew's School in Maryland Episcopla, passion for information technology was growing in the Omidyar. After moving to Hawaii to complete eighth grade and ninth grade, Omidyar has returned to Washington to complete the curriculum.

From an early age, Omidyar was very passionate and small electronic appliances. In third grade, Omidyar have the opportunity to own a computer first - a TRS - 80 with only 4KB of memory. Since then, Omidyar seek ways to spend time and learn computer programming.

After graduating from high school, Omidyar studied computer science at Tufts University and graduated in 1988. There is no excellence in education, Omidyar is not too hard to find a job after graduation. His first job was at Claris, a division of Apple Computer. Here, Omidyar worked for software development projects for the Macintosh and Macdraw. This work has helped him in a position to live with passion computer. But the entrepreneurial potential cause him to not stay there long.

Omidyar said that the most important factors deciding the success is his passion: "In the software field, passion is more important than anything else. I was really inspired by the idea of creating software can provide a benefit or make a positive impact for people. You must believe in what they are doing and really passionate about the things that they can spend enough time and effort to to succeed. " Talking about Omidyar, many analysts believe the path to his success is built on the following factors:

Confidence: Omidyar was a dare to take risks, take risks. He is willing to give a stable job to pursue an idea that many thought would never be possible. Omidyar always consistent with the strategic vision, its objectives and believe that their efforts are rewarded.

Passions: From the small, Omidyar has said that his biggest passion is computers and there is no stopping him to pursue that passion.

Preparation: Difficult one would have expected eBay can grow so quickly in just a few years after its establishment. Omidyar even myself too, but he is always ready for his company's position can grasp any opportunity that may be.

Consistency: Although undergoing many vicissitudes, the pressure is quite large due to fierce competition in the market and skepticism from many sides, Omidyar always persevere in pursuit of his company to go into public. "You can fail in some respects, certain areas, but these are learning experiences are valuable to help you move on. The challenges and this failure is what helps you cope with the difficulties and new challenges "- Omidyar share.

Share the success of Alibaba.com

Birth to the new network and this is Taobao.com

Alibaba.com - Online auction site No. 1 in China, Jack Ma is considered the father of IT industries in the most populous country in the world today.

Jack Ma was born in 1960 in Hangzhou, China in a family whose father was head of a troupe said his mother was a factory worker of watchmaking. From the baby, Jack Ma is very keen to learn English. He can revel in self-learning times for hours talking with foreign tourists in front of their hotel and ready to take the city to visit for free.

In 1981, Jack Ma at the University of Hangzhou Teachers, Faculty of English. After graduation, Jack Ma stay in school and teaching English.
Like most people fluent in foreign languages in China, meanwhile, Jack Ma to teach a lot, especially during very popular in English.

Jack Ma goes later translated. For additional income, he has established a separate office translation. Can speak English capital thanks to its very pretty, Jack Ma has a completely stable income.

But he did not want to stop there. Exposure to many businesses, as Jack Ma is more determined than business.

Formed ideas.

In 1995, once led business delegations to USA, Jack Ma was the first to know and Internet access. American experts said that could exploit the information about the business over the Internet but not necessarily to take place to spend kem.Tuy course, Jack Ma was disappointed to learn that there is no information about Chinese business network transmission. The establishment of websites offering information on Chinese companies from which suddenly appeared.

Return home, Jack Ma wrote abruptly resign teaching. He was a friend borrowed $ 2,000 and jump right into designing a web page. Objects of this site will be the Chinese enterprises are looking for foreign partners. He sought to contact the Ministry of Foreign Trade to gather first information on businesses in need of international trade. Considered a pioneer of business-tech but surprisingly Internet business tycoon Jack Ma did not hide his back is actually a pagan.

However, because of relatively close relationships with a number of American businesses in America when he served as interpreter for them also helped Jack Ma has the necessary support, especially on Internet technology.

Jack Ma's site is also open to provide information to the Chinatown business with each other, also known as B2B information (Busines to Busines). Can tell, the site of Jack Ma is one of the first website to appear in China. Jack Ma drunk with their new products and his tireless work, each day approximately 16 hours.

In the early years, the site of Jack Ma, very few people registered as members. Simple things as the Internet and websites such as this is considered a luxury, especially unfamiliar to most Chinese companies. But Jack Ma did not hesitate to recruit 24 staff working for them.
Calling for investment capital.

In the times to America, Jack Ma has promptly recognized that website provides information about the business model for B2B business as he is doing a great risk of failure. Therefore, Jack Ma had decided to focus on small and medium enterprises. Main small and medium enterprises newly set up boom of private enterprises in the late 1990 onwards as well as the potential partners that foreign businesses are interested in learning. With the new direction that Jack Ma is determined to build a website providing information about the business. But once again, Jack Ma is need for investment capital. Mobilize private capital and their relatives, friends, Jack Ma is only $ 60,000 complete integrity.
Before such a situation, determined to call Jack Ma investment. From the beginning I identified the less capital, which should not even be the only tool for which he is called negotiation business ideas and plans meticulously and he outlines feasible due ra.Da participated in many trade negotiations as also in English translation, so Jack Ma has a lot of experience negotiating. Acquaintances and had talks with Jack Ma has recognized financial speaks very clever and he's convinced. Main so that Jack Ma has persuaded a

venture capital fund's investment firm Goldman Sachs to contribute $ 5 million capital support for the company was Alibaba.com first issue of shares of this enterprise to the public.

"Oh Sesame open doors"

Alibaba, Jack Ma's name was chosen because he wanted that information your site will be a timeless treasure of information and invaluable for every business, similar tales to popular mantra English "Oh Sesame opened." Jack Ma newly established business but who knew he was a visionary. He was not too focused on revenue earned by brokers or provide information to businesses that focus on customer numbers. Many information services are provided free Alibaba.com. Thus the number of member companies joined Alibaba.com rise very fast.

The success of the enterprise through the support of information is the success of Alibaba.com. It was the business perspective of Jack Ma. A big advantage is Jack Ma's Alibaba.com has built web pages simultaneously in both English and Chinese. E-commerce tycoon Jack Ma has already become one of the world's dollar billionaires after mission 35% stake sale of the company Alibaba.com for Yahoo Group.

It is a special event has attracted the attention of the media in 2005. Accordingly, there can know that this is an investment contract has a maximum value of foreign corporations into the Chinese market.

Jack Ma has collected about $ 1.7 billion for Alibaba.com in which 1 billion in cash in exchange for Yahoo to hold 35% stake in Alibaba.com, one of four chairs, along with members of the company's management with nearly 3,000 employees. With sales of more than $ 200 million last year, the youth of this country have for several years was called the idol of their business.

Expand cooperation

Next, Jack Ma did not difficult to be a partner of Japan's Softbank to invest $ 20 million. Jack Ma has used this money to open the online auction site Taobao.com China's largest.

Currently, this site has more than 10 million members and is considered the biggest rival of the online shopping site, the largest in the world today is eBay.

With online auction site Taobao.com names of Alibaba.com and its founder Jack Ma has officially crossed the border in China. He stood in groups of 50 faces that affect the development of the Internet by PC World voted. An interview with CNN, Jack Ma confidently predict that the potential population of 137 million Internet users today, in 10 years, one out of three Internet companies leading the world will belong to his country.

A little information related to Alibaba's e-commerce in

China:
Alibaba.com (Chinese: 阿里巴巴 - A Li Ba Ba) with the slogan "Global Trade starts here ..." is a company e-commerce / online auction was founded in 1999 by Ma Yun (Jack Ma), based in Hangzhou.

English language website alibaba.com specializes in B2B commerce, especially for international customers want to trade with the sale of Chinese visitors. Chinese Website chinese.alibaba.com focus on domestic B2B market in China and www.taobao.com C2C is a commercial site for Chinese customers.

August 11, 2005, Alibaba.com and Yahoo announced an agreement on establishing a long-term strategic partner in China. Accordingly, Yahoo will contribute part of Yahoo China trade to Alibaba.com and the two sides will work together as partners to promote exclusive Yahoo subsidiary in China. Additionally, Yahoo will invest $ 1 billion to buy stake in Alibaba.com, or about 40% to 35% of shares voting, making Yahoo to become the largest strategic investor of Alibaba. com.

As of January 2007, Alibaba Group, composed of 5 companies:

Alibaba.com: Website serving the international trade of

Taobao - eBay's main rival in China on the online auction. Currently Taobao has over 65% of the auction market.

AliPay - the main competitor to PayPal online payment in China.
Alisoft - Activities from January 2007, Alisoft provide web services to market small and medium enterprises.

The story of the founder of Build-A-Bear

Maxine Clark is truly a man who dared to think. She had quit work in order to successfully build their own business, Build-A-Bear company and ready to face the difficulties and challenges.

About Build-A-Bear

Since the establishment of its first store in St. Louis in 1997, Build-A-Bear has grown by 300 stores across Asia,

Canada, Europe and America, with revenues of 437 million U.S. dollars. Build-A-Bear also owns many shares of Ridemakerz - an automotive retailer of toys.

Her story

Upon graduation in 1971 Georga, I thought he wanted to become a lawyer. I subscribe to a lawyer's training school and have to work extra to cover fees. However, everything completely changed when I stepped into the retail sector.

I started learning about this area in May Department Stores in Washington. From a personnel training, I gradually became a manager. At 19, I was involved in all stages from planning, market research to product development. In 1992, I became president of Payless.

Payless ShoeSource leaving, if the financial terms, I might even retire. But I give her a break feeling bored and realized that money makes people only really comfortable when they are doing what they like with it. And I had intended on a new business idea and go back to their customers. I want to apply my experience has been collected to do something really different and unique.
The idea formed to Build-A-Bear on a summer day in 1996. I went shopping with Katie, then she was 10 years

old. We want to buy Bear Beanie Babies, but the store no longer exists. I looked at Katie and said, "Well, we can do well is easy." You mean she is we can make a teddy bear, but I thought further, and the idea of Build -A-Bear Workshop was born like that.

According to my experience, working with passion for what they will bring excitement and motivation for creative work. I do not like to always stick to the old ways of doing new things that are very highly.

For example, at first we did not have business ideas but then I watched Teddy the potential of this work. Some people wonder: "Why did not I think of this?" That is the charm, teddy bears is not something they enjoy.

I have had a lot of errors. But for me, we can learn a lot from their errors. I often encourage others to take a little risk could even make mistakes. But the true failure is the mother of success.

Finally, you let yourself dream, and dream big. Do not limit yourself. Let's dream and believes he can achieve what we want.

Creativity in the business of a Vietnamese-American

Bill Nguyen, the business software millionaire, is now

appearing on the media with variable site lala.com ambition to become a supermarket selling the world's largest music CDs.

200,000 members and more ...

Five years ago, a huge legal battle erupted when people began using the original Napster to swap music online. Now it has launched a new service for owners of multiple CD purchase them. Megan Streich was looking to buy a CD for $ 1 USD. She www.lala.com website where owners of the CD albums listed, but they need to introduce and offer

American Association of recording statistics: every year about 30,000 CD titles shipped. Meanwhile, only about 5,000 CD titles in the store inventory system is the largest retailer Wal-Mart, which is always ready to provide 3 million different CD titles. That, means that only a short time, a large number of titles that drives away the music fans looking for the number of discs in circulation less difficult. Bill Nguyen looks at these numbers and think of a neat way to solve the problem. He co-founded the site to help

fans lala.com CD transaction is more favorable.

A test version of this online service after only a few

months has attracted nearly 100,000 people participating members, and about 200,000 more people ready to join team members when the site was put into operation mode. When Lala was just starting to take a month, there were few people use it to trade nearly 400 CDs.

Bill Nguyen is causing the attention of record labels in the U.S. to turn the project site lala.com become the focal point for the intermediate players everywhere can exchange the old CDs with each other, by the method of exchange Similar types of eBay, at a cost of 1 USD only came up with 49 cents cash plus shipping. This service works as follows: each member will be uploading a list of CDs they have, and other members also see this information.

Each person re-established a list of CDs they want (Want list). When members see a list of other members a CD in the CD in the Want list, they will be able to click on the "wanted" beside the CD in their list Want list. LaLa command will ask all members of the said CD and the first to agree to exchange the CD it will provide the address of the need to transfer them via CD delivery services of LaLa. After receiving confirmation of CD in good condition, they will pay a total fee of LaLa is $ 1.49. Among them, about 20-30 cents is paid to the company, while 20 cents is paid into another fund used to pay copyright for the copyright owner, delivery charge is 49 cents and the rest will belong to the with CD.

Notably, the network promised lala.com deduct 20% of

profits to support artists through charities "Z Fund." "The time may also plenty of old CDs piled in the closet - if people can exchange the CD then there must be good!" - Bill Nguyen said excitedly. Bill said he got the idea to build this site when viewing Wikipedia online dictionary - by the dictionary user-edited. Exchange sites is also a CD of his system work with similar principles.

Megan Streich, online CD sellers, said: "I only spend 1 to 2 hours on the network to pass on all that their CD collections with them and ask questions. Others have begun to use personal website (blog). If she found what she needed, all you need to do is just click of a mouse. She started the trade when someone wants a CD from her collection. "

Constantly looking for success

Bill Nguyen said Lala is bringing a music store the old style. This is good for music fans and artists. Bill Nguyen said: "On the Internet there LaLa all collections, although you are not the Rolling Stones, you're not an artist's reputation, you also have a position in LaLa, where you are hearing author and a group of fans. So we help people discover a new genre. "
Observers commented that this project be combined features of both MySpace.com, eBay.com, and iTunes. Bill Nguyen said: "When you are on our website and

purchase a CD with someone, then you really own a new CD and a CD while you remove your old. So, like eBay or record store Amoeba, you have the right to sell the things you used last. " La La will be selling the CD on the network if an album is no longer used. The seller will provide the CD boxes and envelopes to send goods by post.

Bill Nguyen funny, but always requires people to be themselves and effort

With $ 9 million is poured from the partners are Bain Capital and Ignition Partners, the project was a challenge Lala sent to the companies providing online digital music as Napster. Bill Nguyen said today lala.com has 1.8 million titles available with different titles and 30,000 new listings added every day, able to meet the needs of music in all genres . Source disk is provided by the distributor Baker Taylor, plus contributions from registered members of LaLa service users across the globe. The ambition of the Bill as "shaking hands" with the major record label to dominate the market share of digital music.

35-year-old millionaire has not changed the way people dress casual like early age of welding. Me playing games and giggles a lot, Bill Nguyen is a fun job but always demanding of yourself and others to very high effort. When asked Bill Nguyen - who never graduated from college - the secret of his business, Bill is only short but significant: "Whenever you embark on a new deal, not necessarily you have to play reinvent the world. " In other words, Bill Nguyen says, "standing on the shoulders of giants" should he come so fast.

As a "rookie" in the music business, but in Silicon Valley, Bill Nguyen is too well known. 30 years old, he is in the hands of six different software companies and on the list of 40 richest people under 40 years old United States after a series of fabulous deal. In particular, not to mention the Bill are easy to sell $ 850 million when the company specializes in software OneBox messaging established by him in 1999.

In 2000, Bill found time telephone companies invested billions of dollars on wireless services, Bill trendy "birth" Seven companies, specializing in business software used for mobile services email. Bill immediately raised $ 34 million capital contribution from its partners and immediately Seven companies reap success in the marketplace. Seven's software is used widely and won many prestigious awards including Product of the Year Award by Network Magazine magazine poll. Seven also gained lucrative contract with Microsoft. Extending beyond the U.S. market, the software company Seven were two groups in the UK British Telecom and NTT DoCoMo in Japan, bought the rights to use.

Bill is not the type who prefer sleeping on the win, so he rushed into the new project. He is spending money and need to save any money poured into the project. For years, he never slept more than 4 hours per day. Bill promised worked tirelessly to achieve our goal, to profit from L La and extract the words to help these musicians are still struggling with the living. "MTV Artist ride all that nice to stay home, not everyone can actually be so." Bill himself before becoming a millionaire must strive by selling old cars.

In the opinion of experts, it is too early to confirm the flourishes of lala.com by this site only officially went into operation earlier this month 6-2006. However, Bill is confident in his intuition and he hopes the name Lala - two hours first thing Bill said his son babbles - will bring good luck to him.

Portrait of two founders of Yahoo

Jerry Yang and David Filo is the pioneer in creating a site with many special features to millions of people around the world began a journey on the Internet by clicking on the "menu" of Yahoo.

In 1994 at Stanford University, two graduate students Jerry and David began avidly surfing the web and Yahoo launched to help those of you at Stanford University to locate other sites. Filo said that back then, every day there are thousands of websites launched two people tried to gather all those sites and reorganize them in a way most beneficial to Internet users. At that time, Filo 30 years of age, has led the software development company Yahoo.

Yang and Filo hired a home supervisor for themselves - Sir Tim Knoogle, their classmates at Stanford University and a leader of several high technology companies in the south-west England industry. Upon receiving the offer of Yahoo, Knoogle did not hesitate and immediately accepted the invitation to chair the board.

Yahoo has a total of 14 "items" including Arts (Arts), Economics (Business), Entertainment (Entertainment), Health (Health)..., and especially Yahoo Mail. There are about 120 people to join with Yahoo page executive Jerry Yang and David Filo. Their job is classified websites, advertising.

There are over 350 registered companies advertising trenYahoo!. The reason these companies choose Yahoo because they were convinced by the number of Yahoo users worldwide, and large and by creative new advertising models fully effective . Among Yahoo's customers are Honda and Disney.
However, with Jerry Yang, the success in the future depends on Yahoo's ability to change from the creative site into a "family" of your own media products.

Currently, the company Yahoo increasingly competitive and strong growth. Yahoo's competitiveness began to be appreciated as it is on par with the world's biggest names such as Ted Turner, Bill Gates or Tom Brokaw.

The story of King Car America

The car has remained a symbol of civilized life. The growth and booming car is also a positive expression of a modern industrial age. And the car comes to history is to talk about Henry Ford.His name associated with the birth and development of automobile industry. Henry Ford was named the king of American cars. Ford Car Group is still today one of the group producing the world's largest car factory with millions of vehicles per year and revenue up to hundreds of billions of dollars.

Through many ups and downs with the economy, Ford group cars are still one of the industry group the most important of America. Shares of corporations is one of the participating shares stock market's oldest, most stable. Since two decades Ford family members no longer live reputation in power management group as before. But in defense of traditional corporations, in celebration, people never forget to remind the family names that "Henry Ford.

Not only that, Henry Ford was mentioned as a technical genius and is a talent management industry.

From her famous.

Henry Ford is the son of a farmer is derived from the Icelandic immigration to the U.S. from the early 19th century. He was born in 1863 and is the eldest son among six children of William Ford grandparents. From the small boy Henry proved extremely hyperactive and often mischievous Veiled is.

Living in farm families, but Henry never showed little interest and attachment to their fields or livestock. Conversely, are you curious about all kinds of equipment and machinery. Mr. and Mrs. Ford were many times very frustrating when many household goods were boys loose parts. Unlike the other kids had, the most popular toys of Henry Ford is the saws, hammers, pliers and screw the bowl-sized lots.

It is said that, first saw his father watches, such as Henry was attracted to it. He asked to borrow for it and then sneaked into the room to watch that every intricate detail parts of Wind the clock seconds. Where to go, too, that where there are machines and equipment is what Henry Ford was demanding to see by. See trains run by steam locomotives, Henry Ford's time to learn and determined to do a similar test.

Henry was once feared as the field test than falling off a steam engine running in order to create the campus. The engine blew up, but Henry, the boy satisfied with the products of his early experiments. When he was a new elementary school. Desire to learn and invent techniques are very large differences that people easily recognize him at Henry Ford is curious and playful.

Always haunted by the engine

Later, growing up to do, where Henry Ford also made people amazed and admire the ingenuity and technical talent of his magic. Although made in a wood shop or a mechanic shop, Henry Ford always think about mechanization and motors of the equipment. Perhaps he was meaning of the steam engine from pursuing small anywhere, anytime.

Henry was the main designed a lawn mowing machines and tractors with engines first. Unlike steam engines powered by coal, railways, engines can be run by Henry Wood. So that his product is very suitable and useful for farmers and artisans, small mechanic. Passion to learn and explore, Henry continues to gradually improve the lawn mower and tractor. The number of machine parts more and more, making the machine more powerful and more gadgets. Ideas and models of cars are also formed on that basis.

After years of searching and testing, in the summer of 1896, Henry Ford finished car ran its first steam. Whether to run only on 10km/gio speed and inability to go backwards or turn around, but the test car is a feat Henry Ford shocked the public opinion at the time. Have another two years before Henry Ford had successfully made car is quite simple but fully functional to the road.

Immediately, Henry Ford had a contract placed first in his life. Detroit Post Office has ordered four vehicles for the transport of parcels.

Become a car manufacturer.

Since 1902, the new Ford car company was officially born. Henry Ford was associated with a professional business enterprise to finance coal company. From there, he began hiring workers to manufacturing and assembling machines themselves, not just tinkering design, fabrication and assembly just like the first few cars. Purchase orders are more and more that Henry was forced to think about the specialization of production stages.

If at the Henry Ford could build cars according to specific requirements of each client, now he has switched to the more standardized parts of the car. There are new parts that meet the huge demand for purchase by customers. Besides technical innate talents that blessed him, the qualities of an industrial managers have begun to form in the person of Henry Ford.

Henry Ford directly responsible for designing and operating production also his partner dedicated to the sales process. Is a technique born, Henry Ford himself never satisfied with their cars. He still ply drunk with car models with improved quality. Hundreds, then thousands of improvements were made in a few years. Ford cars increasingly stronger, faster, more relevant and even more beautiful was born.

In total over the past five years have up to 8 different generation Ford was born. On that basis, Henry Ford had built a very successful group most modern cars. Ford is now the car stood Group 2 in U.S. vehicle sales up to a hundred billion dollars a year.
Ad welcoming customers.

During this time, the market has pretty much matched its cars, Ford is no longer unique position as the first, most cars are still too expensive for many people at that time.

Market pressures have forced Henry Ford to calculate the specific business strategies. And he has decided to choose a direction that no one daring to do. Ford is a popular type of car, for all subjects. That business philosophy of the founder of the Ford company still maintained to this day. Henry Ford invested in a large factory, expanding the chain to be highly specialized in order to lower the cost of shipping the vehicle.

On the other hand, he actively used the mass media to promote Ford to make cars with ordinary objects. For the first time this many people still think Henry Ford was a technical genius. But not only that, unexpectedly, he has proven himself as a keen businessman with a commercial marketing is very unique at that time. Simmering determination to produce a lot of cars, sold so many, in all classes was motivated Henry Ford to have the creativity in business.

Never studied or trained in methods of marketing, but suddenly in a very short time, the inventor of the flower car proved to be equally excellent in selling. Automobile factory expansion is not done, the popular car models only in design but Henry Ford has boldly introduced to the public. He directly referred to each potential customer. Henry Ford at the same time actively organized many conference presentations Ford automobile products.

All these marketing efforts today are very ordinary, but exactly 100 years ago it was an event, a very bold idea. Henry Ford tried to contact and create a good relationship with the press and the media to advertise their cars and the results achieved are very satisfactory. When the popular line of Ford cars began operating the car factory which is now being sold that car.

Thousands of units have been sold in the first year of the

Ford model T, the popular new vehicles launched, but has received very warmly. Difference whether the profitability of these vehicles is not high, there is relatively low period over another, but in return Henry Ford "eaten" by the numbers. Yet it was reasonably priced, good quality with ingenious marketing strategies without any long-lived line of vehicles such as vehicles.

Exist exactly two decades, total car company of Henry Ford has sold hundreds of Ford model T car with enough different colors.
People who know how to find and keep.

There are skilled staff, has mastered the difficult, but keep them even harder in an environment of free competition. In the 20-30 years of the 20th century, there are many more than the Ford car company newly established in the U.S.. So the competition and keep most managers and workers, good employees is not easy.

Henry Ford is well aware that their profits have been made and by workers. Therefore, he has shown much attention to the development of a treatment regime and appropriate compensation for workers. Noteworthy point is that Henry Ford made entirely from the thought of themselves not necessary as the pressure from outside. This is different from a business standpoint maximum profit of the Emerging capitalism.
Henry Ford actually was paying attention to profits, has the right business toward profitability, as much as

possible. But Henry Ford was to look very far. He soon hunches and predictions about the shortage in the labor market and high skilled. Therefore the salary of workers at Ford have a significantly higher share than in other companies. That is not including social benefits other voluntary Henry Ford also voluntarily for their employees.

With the business philosophy and use of such people, Henry Ford transformed the work at each position his company to become honorable. And each one of the workers here are secure and proud of his company. Henry Ford himself thus can safely continue to invest in expanding production systems of their Ford cars.

YouTube story.

Time magazine has voted the website YouTube "Invention of the Year 2006." The birth of this website has created a film trend - online video.
2006 was an exciting era in technology. Nintendo

invented a new games that gamers can control wand. A new car was invented and ran to 1330 km with one liter of gasoline. A robot can learn to drive. But only YouTube created a new way for millions of people in the world of entertainment, learning and shock at a level that we have not seen before. Most remarkable, the founder of YouTube only about two little old.

In 2004, during a party in Silicon Valley, three-man Steve Chen, Chad Hurley and Jawed Karim chat about they can easily share pictures with friends online, but extremely difficult to transfer video on the Internet. Then they started to develop this idea. They try all kinds of video formats can be uploaded to any web browser on any computer. They built a kind of virtual village filled with videos, a website where anyone can upload their footage together to view, marking together, sharing together comment and watch other people can find What or video. So YouTube was born.
But the trio did not really understand that they have created a breakthrough even though they were built website. They think they simply created a useful tool for people to share travel videos. They think people only use this website to offer for sale on eBay. They absolutely had no idea about the breakthrough that they have created, the door opened a movement to change the background of the online entertainment world.

As soon as people saw YouTube they are attracted to this website and 'help' for those who created the website to recognize the true value: they spin this website!

Instead of uploading home videos, people threw up their YouTube videos drunk drunk, fell down skiing ... They go online to send the crazy idea they invented, the songs they composed or simple performance than the simple dogma that they clone the famous singer. They posted pictures true thing they recorded, from the devastating storms in News Orleans to the war in Baghdad - from both sides. They published the theory of conspiracy. They sat in the basement alone and mind the unspoken secrets of their privacy with the webcam. YouTube suddenly resounding success even without a business plan which was outlined earlier. Just started with a video of the zoo trip since April last year, YouTube now has over 100 million video clips and other members posting about 70,000 videos each day!

The website founder began developing their companies more seriously. In late 2006, they moved the small office of 30 people to own a building in California, after selling the company to Google for $ 1.65 million more, YouTube also associated with television channels, studios, music labels such as NBC, CBS, Universal Music, Sony BMG and Warner Music to resist posting the clips are not copyrighted. Website start making a lot of money from ads and now they're doing more in terms of improved procedures for use on the website and help users protect their copyright works and can make money by posting videos by the users perform. Therefore, a generation 'filmmakers' network' is about to be formed soon. With YouTube, everyone has the opportunity to become

The story of the founder of USA Today

In 1982, when the newspaper first published in USA Today, who founded it - Allen Neuharth has been Wall Street analysts and reporters laughed. Today, USA Today has become famous names, ranks second worldwide in number of pages written in English

 The initial objective of the paper is to provide a national newspaper for information the U.S. market, at which time virtually the only local newspaper of general circulation.

Color and bold, with lots of charts, large photos, newspaper opposition to completely black and white contemporary newspapers such as The Wall Street Journal and The New York Times. Focus on national objectives, a USA Today newspaper has become known for a huge audience, are distributed across 50 states in the country and ranked second worldwide in the ranking of pages English language.

Allen had previously built a chain of regional newspapers local very successful, so why did you decide to continue publishing a newspaper that only last glance it was possible that it contains so many Risk? Who will need this paper?

Until now, the answer to this question is clear, millions of people are reading newspapers and will continue to read it, but at the time in 1982, when the newspaper was first shown to the public, not everyone can find the answer.

Allen saw the future for the chain of his family's newspaper that others can not. He also saw the desire seeking information about the complex issues of readers. Based on newspaper distribution network in the area, Allen has created a delivery process meticulously reported, including periods in newspapers and distributed national newspaper. So what has allowed Allen can foresee the ability to successfully develop a national newspaper? That's because he owns a strategic vision, ability to anticipate trends and future development of the more important is the ability to turn this vision into reality.

Ability to recognize the future potential of an organization or company is always a crucial factor for the success of the leadership. Actually, when certain characters are considered "great leader", the automatic response of humans is something that cited the possibility of strategy or vision of these leaders.

We often hear stories of successful CEOs in history and it is definitely attached to their strategic capabilities. The failure of many CEOs of multi-rooted weakness or lack of visionary leadership style. However, a proper and correct vision that is not easy. Allen's vision of a national newspaper seems very reasonable in today's stage, but at the time in 1982, it seems to be ... impractical.

It is clear that vision has affected directly, both established in historical context. Vision separate historical context can produce surprising results. An unreasonable period of the 1920s and the explosion of the Internet era in the 1990s is testament to the vision that is sometimes not based on fact. These great leaders just need to grasp opportunities in line with the current context has always had the potential plans for the future . Although context is important in the process of setting a firm foundation for success, but the leaders are not passive in this context. Leaders such as Allen and could have created the parameters for success through a sound vision for the future. And most importantly, as mentioned above, they possess the ability to see the prospect of a possible vision.
...

The foundation of leadership vision.

Theodore Hesburgh, Rector of the University of Notre

Dame said that "The essence of leadership is that you must have a vision. It is a vision that you encrypt a clear and powerful from time to time. "

Leaders share a dream and direction that others want to share and follow. Leadership vision goes beyond the tasks required to complete the company's annual or individual leaders. Vision leadership permeates the workplace and is reflected in the actions, beliefs, values and goals leader.

Most of the businesses or any business which will begin with a vision of what the founders saw that it could create. Share this vision with others in a way to get others to act to realize the vision is the key to a successful leadership vision, a leader successful because, as mentioned above, almost as seen at the time vision, that vision is easily seen as a silly thing.

Here are some of the foundations necessary to encourage and attract others to follow the vision that leaders have seen before. They are:

- Set goals and clear organizational direction.

- Inspire loyalty and interest through calls for the participation of everyone.

- Demonstrate and reflect the strengths, culture, values, beliefs and orientations of individual companies.

- How to subordinates always see that they are part of something larger than themselves. Challenges subordinates to know: Sometimes they go to try things beyond their reach.

Who created the phenomenon of Wikipedia.

Jimmy Wales is best known as the founder of Wikipedia. He started this project with a friend named Larry Sanger in 2001 and considers it a hobby of his.

Wikipedia now has become a library's largest encyclopedia in human history. Information from this site has been used for more than 100 court decisions in the U.S. since 2004. But Wikipedia may just be the start of Wales. Recently, he began to operate the search engine of its own called Wikia Search, only to find the sites mentioned in Wikipedia.

Wikipedi, written in many languages and is one of 20 sites most visited. However, the most striking features of Wikipedia is that visitors are invited to contribute articles and edit information is available on site for accuracy.

According to Wales, there are so many people should read contents of incorrect information will soon be rectified. However, there are many opinions doubt on the accuracy and objectivity of the site if it is just the result of voluntary contributions.

This method was criticized a lot, even from Sanger, who co-founded Wikipedia. Accuracy and plagiarism is a concern and worry most about the site, but Wales insisted that the policy of self-editing Wikipedia is no different policies in the organization of information.

Wales said: "The newspaper has an editor who edited and fast. We do not know who they are, but we always believe they do a good job. This is how our work in Wikipedia. "

In fact, Wikipedia has been the subject of deliberate sabotage is calculated, the heated discussions between the corrected information and jokes. Some reports, including all of Wales, has been classified as restricted editing. Need to add that particular statement in the history of Wales website has been revised to 18 times.

However, Wikipedia has become a phenomenon and Wales has established the Wikimedia Foundation to look at the future expansion of their business online. Wales also has expanded into several models Wiki other projects, including Wiktionary, Wikinews, and for-profit company Wikia (founded 2004). Wales is becoming more prestigious and Time magazine selected as one of the

100 who made the world. "

The key to free education.
Actually, online job searching is only part of the Wales job. The purpose of this is to everyone on the planet free access to huge volumes of knowledge in human history and gives them a tool to further their own discoveries.

Wales said: "Think of a system of free education to all network resources available to everyone anywhere in the world. If this is reserved for third world countries, the result is great. "

Online encyclopedia, is one factor that constitutes the Wikimedia Foundation. This is a charity with the presence of all the business activities of nonprofit Wales, which includes a reference to dictionaries, lists of species and free libraries named Wikibooks. According to Wales, "Wikibooks is a very interesting field and is a key to the idea of free education. The ultimate goal is to give the book to any college course in the world. "

However, to achieve this, Wales said that governments around the world to rewrite copyright law. Wales believes that the documents must be filed within 14 years of copyright, like in America. When the time expires, the author must be permitted to continue to hold the next 14 years of copyright, by registering with the government and pay a small fee.

"Thanks to this, what is the economic value will continue

to be protected by copyright because they deserve a fee. What no economic value but may have cultural values or education will be ranked in the property allows the public to certain agreements. "

Wales also runs a trading company for profit, called Wikia. This idea has attracted hundreds of millions of dollars funding from Amazon and 4 million in cash from a group of famous people in Silicon Valley.

Wales is different, but successful people in the internet era. He lived very simply in a Florida suburb, a Silicon Valley thousands of miles. He has to earn enough money as a seller of goods and can live comfortably for the rest of his life.In rare spare time, Wales prefer picking in the garden and felt very happy to discover that it was a huge round melons. The meantime, Wales now feel that I should write this again because "this dish really lemony. Only then will we know how to make lemonade."

Meebo and stories about the founders.

Two years ago, Meebo is a name familiar to the online community. But now, every 10 Internet users admit they have used nine service instant messaging technology Ajax. But no one knows some component Meebo founder only 3 people, all very young.

They are often people known as "triple Meebo, including a boy named Seth Sternberg and two girls: Sandy Jen, Elaine Wherry.

CEO and co-founder Seth Sternberg site Meebo.com 28 years old, "elderly" in the group. Meebo trio that success is so incredible on their own. Seth Sternberg modest: "We just think that it will simply help people solve personal problems.

Meebo is the instant messaging service using Ajax technology was born on 4/9/2005. Meebo users means users can log into any site, any electronic messaging such as AIM, ICQ, Yahoo Messenger or MSN Messenger or other networks such as Google Talk uses Jabber ...

Meebo is available approximately 50 languages, including Vietnamese. Maybe so, but every day there is more than 90 million electronic messages through Meebo and implementation of the 5.5 million people use the service each month.

"Meebo's name does not mean anything special. Simply because it is easy to read, easy to remember names and not touching any other online service. It happened when we came up with a meal at the restaurant California

Before embarking together on a project to create, all three women worked in large and reputable companies in the U.S.. Seth Sternberg former IBM employee, but why leave the company to pursue his Meebo is very simple: "In re IBM, I found that my contribution is negligible compared to other employees. A start the new top team, your company completely new is exactly what we aim to young people. "

Together to create something that dreams and aspirations of the three unknown date. When the idea of Meebo appear, they knew that I had something to pursue, to pour effort and hope to ...

How the group "marketing" service Meebo is classified as unique and equally desperate. Instead of having to source funding, fundraising fiscal first and then develop their products as people have done before, this third release of their products into society as soon as completed, then then create a blog (online diary) to "langxe" product and receive feedback from users. "We believe that in such a way, donors and investors will actively seek to group", Elaine Wherry said. "And then we got venture capital money hefty investment from Sequoia Capital Company with a fairly comfortable psychologically. Our children have many opportunities to start again. If not dared to challenge the new failure is the failure ...".

Sternberg decisively: "Never regret to have to give the desirable location is touted by leading companies. When you are working with a project to build by yourself, you will end your life because of it, but never regret. "

Lessons from Fred DeLuca, founder of the Subway. Today, Subway has been in the hands of more than 30,000 stores in over 91 countries around the world, ahead of MacDonald's. But when Fred DeLuca opened shops selling burgers in Bridgeport, Connecticut (USA), he is simply a struggling student trying to earn extra money to pay tuition fees for universities.
Fred DeLuca family moved every few years in one place, and the third time they moved to Bridgeport, Connecticut. Fred DeLuca high school here and applied to study medicine at Bridgeport in general to get a plate with a doctor, but financial difficulties caused him to think how to make caps tuition. DeLuca would like to do business in iron stores, but the meager wages of $ 1.25 dollars per hour as the salt out of sea indeed.

In due time, Fred DeLuca family received a call from longtime friend Mr. Pete Buck, then just changed jobs and moved over near the city. Buck DeLuca appointment to the game. And in the afternoon on Sunday, in July 1965 was memorable, Pete Buck pulled out of his pocket a newspaper article about Mike Davis, owner of a restaurant system.

Article "Mike started empty-handed, so that 10 years later, he was boss of the whole system 32 stores." Talked for a while, Buck suggested that DeLuca should open a shop selling bread sandwiched meat, only that you have the enough money to pay school fees. DeLuca in the abdomen that this is a weird idea, but he still asked curiously "What should I do?".

Buck explained to the young general principles of a bread shop selling meat clamps. He told DeLuca that he just rented a small shop, designed for sales, purchase, and open the shop, so simple. If DeLuca determination, he will help the initial capital. And before you got up, Buck signed a sheet of card worth $ 1,000 dollars and awarded to DeLuca.

That is the story of the day Sunday. Even on Monday morning, DeLuca was scouring the city to find a reasonable place to shop. Room hire and sales, even to purchase equipment. DeLuca very bright idea, he advertised in local newspapers, "A student should buy the old refrigerator," and that the couple were shopping DeLuca refrigerator can cost $ 10 each.

Had barely opened stores there were closed because the risk of financial trouble. DeLuca discovered that he needed a sink fitted with a special price of $ 550 dollars. Fortunately, Pete Buck silent DeLuca a key for the check worth $ 1,000 dollars more, and work continues to progress.

Last winter the following year, DeLuca opened second store not far way. But both establishments sell bread meat had lost grip. Talk to Pete Buck for a while, DeLuca decided that the best way now is not closed both stores, which is open every Tuesday .... And the result is true, not so long after, DeLuca began collecting the first close.

Frederick A. DeLuca was born in 1948 in Brooklyn, New York, in a family of Italian immigrants. 10 years old, Fred DeLuca know how to make money by collecting empty bottles around the neighborhood. Two cents for a bottle. Today, Subway chain ranked third worldwide in the business of fast food, and is one of the private company's largest multi-national with global annual revenue exceeds 9 billion dollars.

Right from the start to open stores, DeLuca has been set for his purpose: to open 32 stores within 10 years, ie repeat the success of Mike Davis that he published any day.

When you have three stores in hand, think DeLuca continued, the only way to achieve objectives is the franchise (franchising). Work, according to calculations by DeLuca, nothing complicated: recruit, train them and give them an independent business.

DeLuca started this plan by convincing a friend of his trial. A few years later, the number of sandwich shops called Subway began to multiply at breakneck speed. To have 100 stores in 1978, and in just four years later there were 200 new stores open. Companies in 1987 reached 1,000 stores. Since then, annual average 1000 Subway to open new stores.

The lessons of DeLuca.

Lesson No. 1: Start the Full "was the strange children" were also normal.
History of the Subway success shows us something interesting that a business can succeed even if he does not have any business knowledge in the field to pursue. When DeLuca opened sandwich shop, he works two jobs that previously had not ever done: business management and processing of meat sandwiched bread.

Before opening its first store, DeLuca and Buck Pete's doing a round of selling sandwich in the state to "study the experiences of colleagues."
They carefully observe every detail, from how to use spices to pouring oil onto frying meat. The initial capital is tight does not allow files to try several plot DeLuca gear head, he must make a product to be sold immediately to customers.

Lesson No. 2: Take out the target to reach, then think about implementing that goal.

From the moment he heard the story of Mike Davis, DeLuca immediately outlined his own plans clear: you must open 32 stores within 10 years. "That was the destination that we set out a very serious way from the beginning" - DeLuca recalls, "We have never hesitated or hesitant about this goal, by contrast, we repeated the such as that of myself - if someone has achieved it, which means we'll do it. "

DeLuca was excited when the building first sandwich shop, a friend reminded him that he must first be approved by the city government plans.The room is designed to DeLuca, immediately drawing sketches in front of government employees, approved and signed.

Lesson No. 3: Put yourself in the position of the customer.

DeLuca always try to figure out if their customers are, you will want to shop like activity. From there he set out the unique ideas.
For example think how he was wheeled out in front of buyers, let them see and be assured that the components of the sandwich has always ensure quality.

DeLuca also must think of the opening of its own bread oven in order to serve its stores, he also is designed to make bread machine, make sure that Subway's bread is healthier than the normal breads.

Matt Mickiewicz Founding SitePoint·

Among web designers and web programmers who do not know sitepoint, but few know the man behind sitepoint, Matt Mickiewicz.Chung that we learn about the journey and said sitepoint founder Matt Mickiewicz said.
Ten years ago, when only 15 years old, with Matt Mickiewicz and Mark Harbottle trangweb founder and professional based in Melbourne. Two people have developed it into a thriving company that profits earned millions of dollars every year without any one donor. Initial interest was there.

Since its inception, the company earn a profit every month and they actively expanding into the field of printing and branding for the web professional. Not long ago, in August of 2008, Matt developed into 99designs SitePoint, a leading company in the market network design and reappears every 30 minutes a new graphics on the Internet.

Webmaster-Resources.com Matt started, the forerunner of SitePoint in 1998. From personal preferences, the site of Matt's favorite quickly. Not long after, he received the pay offer. At that time, he must decide for yourself or pay or find a business partner to continue development.
Only a few months after birth Webmaster-Resources.com special articles on the network appeared on the Los Angeles Times (LA Times), the United States today (U.S. Today), Washington Times (The Washington Times) and page of the journal WINDOWS.

Unfortunately, when the sheet WINDOWS Magazine has

an article on Matt's website has removed hyphens in the name of the site, a bad sign, said that name did not last long.

Only when investors see the potential.
Meanwhile, Mark has entered the fight with Matt to find a better solution in late 1999. SitePoint name was inspired by the listing market for Microsoft's CarPoint, which Mark Harbottle, Matt's business partner had seen while driving in Melbourne.

They launched in January SitePoint 3 / 2000 and opened an office in Melbourne in the summer of that year.
SitePoint is a company o ¬ nline media and information provider targeting fast-growing web market professionals, especially professional network design.

SitePoint has 479.701 subscribers to believe, a huge number. Company registration e-newsletter four different. Three types out once every two weeks, and focus on three topics: design, graphics or business. Topics to be discussed Wednesday in the online forum. There are five, the main income of the company is advertising and sponsorship activities, products and retail o ¬ nline quality, software, subscription video and make a list of ads in the newspaper.

Matt forums and participate in discussions related to the o ¬ nline sales, marketing and network development. He criticized the website and answer every e-mail messages. He tried to help everyone whenever possible.

In the initial days, with partner Matt never a waste of income. Since they are considered experts in their field of network development is to invite companies to design in Melbourne. They only hire people when they have the income and never get the big projects before they are ready.

Matt's advice for those who want to follow him to sell a product or an essential service that Google can not back down and offered free throughout the 12 months. Find products and services that you can see profits and success, even just 0.5 percent of your potential customers know about your existence.

The sale of the site at the conference has become a market characterized 99designs since birth.

99designs, Matt's brand new company is a competitive market for maximum design graphic design. 99designs connect customers looking for design work for clients such as logo, business cards cards, websites and various other graphics facilities, without the usual risks and difficulties related to problems hiring a freelance designer or a design firm. Matt and Mark never embarked on the idea, but only when investors realize their potential.

Honda: The Story "Great start ..."

Comes to economic development in Japan after the Second World War can not not mention the Honda Group. Comes to brand fame in Japan as the world can not not mention the Honda brand. Honda has become a part of Japan.

The message from the trademark symbol.

Symbol of Honda's brand actually includes two parts: a large letter H in the frame and a wing. No one knows, history can not be present and its founder Soichiro Honda was until he died in 1991 and never once revealed, that's what the wings of birds and the letter H itself had be merely the first letter of their name or not Honda. Just know that this brand icon has several times changed over time. When the letter H was thin, thin, slender, sometimes it bold stout. Both birds too. Early, very long wings, long enough to make sense is that birds have wings does not exist in reality. Later it was collapsing again. Two symbols are used separate from each other, show up at two different locations on its products, but also when grafted together into a common symbol.

Just because there is no formal orientation to explain the meaning of the trademark symbol, so the fans of Honda's products around the world have many different understandings of this icon brand. Do not know their feelings are identical with the idea of the author or trademark symbol, but actually it does not decide, because ultimately, the value and meaning, impact and influence of brand weighed measured at the customers and users is key, but where have the profound implications of the author when creating brand logos.

Honda brand icons such as the presence of Honda's products today officially since 1993. But the letter H characterizes Honda first appeared in 1963 in small type T-360 trucks, and graphics wing is attached to the company's first product when it was established in 1947/1948 - at the bike computer.

Everyone said that the letter H is derived from the name Honda. But the other birds are considered a symbol of dreams and desire to take the wings away and up, has recently virtual truth and simplicity that can contain many messages. Someone explain the letter H for the image icon people stand on their feet, two hands reach out to more glorious achievements of creative labor.

Dream life.

The interpretation is not unfounded because "dreams and aspirations," the role and influence in the life decision of the group founder Soichiro Honda. Was not your first bike that he assembled the year 1947/1948 was the name of "Dream" which stars, but the bike machine that is the starting point of the process of formation and development of the Honda brand.

Soichiro Honda was born on 17/11/1906 in Komyo, a village in central Japan. Right from childhood, Soichiro had helped his father repair bicycles at age 8 and boy was first seen a car. Then, the boy had insisted later built cars like that. Later, Soichiro to Tokyo for training in an automobile workshop text, join manufacture racing and became a very successful racer, along with his brother up racing speed record of 120 km / h which to have destroyed 20 years later in Japan, but then have to retire after an accident. In 1937, Honda established company Tokai Seiki Heavy Industry Co.. Ltd. specializes in manufacturing checks - cement for automobile engines. On it, just to Toyota is the company's customers. His study of metallurgy and metal working to improve and enhance product quality. In 1946, Soichiro Honda established "Honda Technical Research Institute (Honda Technical Research Institute) - heard calling but the fact that only a small bungalow. That is the period immediately after the second world war, the infrastructure was destroyed in Japan, the Japanese were controlled and controlled by the agreement of the allies. Honda has received just that, one of the most urgent needs for the Japanese is the ability to move and transport simple. After acquiring the electric motor 500 by the military emissions, Honda is now the first business idea that simple originality, technical feasibility and economic efficiency is very high, which is to improve bicycle the mopeds. Volume Honda brand development from a small wooden house with her and released her first product. From mopeds, Honda and research institutions to create two-stroke motorcycle engines, motorcycles and four-stroke engine. In 1948, Honda formed Honda Motor Co. Ltd. along with Takeo Fujisawa totaling 1 million yen, the company linked to its original. Only a few years later, the Honda engine has gained 60% market share in Japan. In 1949, the factory Honda bike for its first, is also the first motorcycle was built and assembled entirely in Japan, of course with the name "Dream." In 1955, Honda leads the Japanese market. In 1963, Honda built the first automobile and sports car racing S500, opens a new era. Since it is beyond the boundaries of Honda of Japan to reach out to the world, possibly new products subject to the pinnacle of science and technology such as aircraft or industrial plants. The dream life of Soichiro Honda have come true.

The secret of success.

History of Honda brand is very successful story of a Japanese airline industry. The secret of success first and most important of these brands are welcome trends of the market. Its motto is aimed at what the market currently and in future will need to strive to not only launch what is possible. Honda grows along with the development of the Japanese demands on transportation and travel, from the simplest ones, such as a bicycle computer to create complex achievements such as industrial robots, aircraft, or cell vehicles using solar energy.

The secret of success is that Honda's second utilized the international race to promote themselves and to reach the destination. Speed and convenience, safety and design advertising and marketing is most effective through the participation of motorcycles and race cars as well as through international awards achieved there.

The secret of success is Honda's third focus from the beginning to continuously improve their competitiveness not only in Japan. Fuel efficiency and high power devices to meet the aesthetic demands of consumers and standards-friendly environment in which the set time, reaching out to conquer the market in the continent since the early days . not competing with other giants in their own strengths against their weaknesses ... is what has helped Honda to achieve the things that the other giants of the world must take twice as long to reach be So that the view that dreams and aspirations seems always in front of Honda.

Biography Morihei Ueshiba, the founder of Aikido.

Patriarch Morihei Ueshiba was born on 14/12/1883 in a

small town named Tanabe (1) near Osaka. Patriarch of reconstituted on 26.04.1969. Meanwhile Hombu dojo is a large three-story buildings and Aikido are hundreds of thousands of people enrolled in the five continents. From a boy wasting illness.

Patriarch Morihei Ueshiba was born on 14/12/1883 in a small town named Tanabe (1) near Osaka. He was the fourth son of a yeoman named Ueshiba Yoroku, with a fortune of nearly 20 acres of land. Ueshiba is true in detail Yoroku town council, is also a character name in Tanabe City.

Childhood, Morihei Ueshiba Patriarch was a boy physically weak, or ill feeling and emotion. 7 year old boy type with a Buddhist monk named Fujumoto Mitsujo. At this stage there are often myths are circulated in the Kumano region. These stories by Kobodaishi from China and they narrate a profound impression on his mind Morihei made you gush in disillusionment. His father was worried because the tendency to dream of the boy, and also to enhance his fitness to practice sumo should start Morihei Ueshiba (2) and swimming. In the first years of primary school, he received Morihei impact of teacher training his Tasaburo Nasu, out of both body and spirit. The later became an important figure in the field of religion.

Years to 13 years old boy in high school but only saved Tanabe there for a year because of his hobby is to learn soroban (3). Morihei Ueshiba is particularly gifted in this area and only less than a year later, he advanced to become the assistant trainer. Then he joined the staff duty office Tanabe. There, he is in charge of the temple tax. While doing his job of tax collection also mindful of the problems of farmers and fishermen and feel dissatisfied because their working conditions. He participated in demonstrations demanding reform, change a new law on fisheries identity. After the harsh crackdown, he would resign and to Tokyo. At first, he made a run the vacuum in a wholesale store. In the spring of 1902, Ueshiba rent a booth at Asakusa under Ueshiba Shokai signs (4) for sale of stationery for pupils, students, in the region.

At this time, Ueshiba's attention to the growing martial art. After the store closed, he focused study of the ancient techniques of Jujutsu, especially technical discipline with Masters Kyto Tozawa the same time he also set kenjutsu (5) in a direct line of men's Shinkage (6) . After a few months, Ueshiba Morihei disease emphysema and must return to Tanabe, where the guy's hometown. There, Ueshiba Morihei married to a childhood friend she is Hatsu Itokawa.

Since returning home, Ueshiba Morihei vowed to give his body a muscular, athletic. Hard work he pursued a harsh training and gradual, based on health conditions and muscle forces. At twenty years old, although a little tall (1m54), Morihei had a power over ordinary people very much. But physical strength is not merely satisfy him, so he came to Sakai (7) to learn the discipline of the Yagyu swordsman (8) with teacher Nakai.

In 1903, the situation between Russia and Japan became strained, Ueshiba subscribe to 61 infantry regiments stationed in Osaka. Soon, he became the champion in all the practice and especially the subject Ju jutsu ken (9).

Morihei Ueshiba's regiment was sent to Manchuria fronts. There, the exemplary behavior of the superior man makes note and he was promoted to sergeant. Fighting ability of men wonder that the comrades give him the nickname "Heitai no kami sama" (10). As he was discharged, he advised the commander of the guy on the field to train officers as professional soldiers. Morihei Ueshiba rejected this proposal and to take care of the home farm. During the four years of war, he did not stop practicing martial arts and continues to communicate with master Nakai, Yagyu under sect. Then he received by the sect in 1908.

During this time, Ueshiba Morihei energetic and attentive to issues of politics, society in the region. He set up a facility similar to a club youth activities. Here he set up a judo dojo to train with a masters swim just to live in the city. This position, named Kiyoichi Takagi, later to become the permanent need black belt level.

Become King "Shirataki"

In 1910, the Japanese government wants to exploit migrants and Hokkaido regions should call on volunteers to establish business migrants, Ueshiba Morihei Patriarch realized that the program should be useful to gather a group of 80 people to hit the road as the first colonizers. After a two-month journey, they come to camp in Hokkaido and a place that later became the village of Shirataki. After two years of reclamation and work hard, and they began to reap the fruits and decided to settle there. Patriarch Morihei Ueshiba was a plentiful initiative: he thought that the mint plant, set up a base of forest exploitation. He also invested in cattle, horses, and set up milk processing combinations. With the urging of his people have built up a trade center, a school and a clinic. He has also contributed to the expansion Shirataki Temple.

2 / 1925, during his trip to Engaru, he met with the teachers of the sect called Takeda Daito Sokaku Kubota hotel. Takeda master immediately recognize this young man in a non-ordinary personality and he decided to impart all the secrets of the sect Daito Ryu (11). Although initially only through this visit, Patriarch Morihei Ueshiba decided to prolong and save a

month to practice with his new teacher.

Once back Shirataki, who opened a dojo and invited

Takeda to teach teachers. Who built a house for his teacher and provide for his every need. Upon receiving a special diploma schools of Daito Ryu, the Patriarch was just learning to master Takeda came up with a hundred days. Time left for personal training.

6 / 1918, it was suggested that his election to City Council and he was elected commissioner. Also at that time, due to his initiative, people began to build railroads Hokkaido.

May 11/1919, he received bad news about the health status of the father. So moved, he decided to leave all possessions and with his family back to Tanabe.

On the way back, he heard rumors in the region have a great monk Ayabe have more power spirit named Onisaburo Deguchi, Ueshiba Morihei Patriarch decided to cross back to visit Deguchi master asked him to pray for peace for my father. People feel the need to have this meeting while undergoing trial, because even though I realize that martial arts excellence and vitality, but mental strength is still weak and vague and prone to wobble when meeting a psychological challenge.

His father who died on 2/1/1920 and arrived home just two days later in Tanabe.

The death of his father as Patriarch Ueshiba Morihei was suffering, he's gone through many ups and downs and decided to stay in Ayabe in the temple of the sect

Omotokyo to learn with the guidance of Mr. Deguchi Onisaburo.

Omotokyo is a religion of Shinto is founded Ms. Nao Deguchi. After receiving the divine revelation, has developed a strong cult when her groom is Kitasabuno Ueda (later renamed Deguchi Onisaburo) became the leader. For Omotokyo, identified by the words of Professor Jean Herbert, the "spirit of God is instilled throughout the universe and human beings are stewards ruled heaven and earth. Once people have merged with God, it has been an endless power. Humans are the temple of God and God is also human capital formation. Man and God to make together. "

Omotokyo commanded his followers to follow three precepts to be closer to God:

1. Please observe the phenomena of nature and you will be the nature of heuristics true God.

2. Look at the excellent circulation of the universe and you will experience the power of thought God truth.

3. You look at the minds of the creatures to be aware of the true spirit of God.

Tang first line search.

Deguchi Onisaburo authorities were suspicious and had repeatedly thrown in jail for various reasons, including reasons for the emperor blasphemy and violating the press law. However, he was eager to operate in the social sectors for the elderly, orphans, destitute and in writing. As an advocate of peace, he formed associations to protect love and brotherhood in the world in 1925. He contacted many religions in the world and contribute to the founding of the Federation of religion in the world.

Dated 13/2/1924, although still appointed by the lese majeste residence, he quietly left the country via Japan to Mongolia, along with some disciples, including Patriarch Morihei Ueshiba. They feed dream of building a peaceful kingdom in Mongolia - where the armies of China and Japan are fighting - by creating an alliance between the two camps are based on conquest and the power of the religious new teachers.

They failed in their attempt and the Chinese were arrested. After months of imprisonment and more than once narrowly escaped death, they were assigned to solve for the Japanese government. When introduced to Japan, had a great crowd to applaud when they set foot on the port of Moji in late May 6 / 1925.

Back Ayabe, Patriarch Morihei Ueshiba as more effort in the study of Budo and live a life of austerity. Main at this point, the next a naval officer which is a kendo sensei (direct search) to visit, because he heard the name of. In exchange stories, by disagreement on some points, the visitors suggested Patriarch Morihei Ueshiba billion experiment. Patriarch gave the officer a wooden sword and told him that he does not need to earn. The officer on the attack, but could not be touched him. Tired, he stopped and Patriarch explained to him that he felt before the attack just before his prime work. He saw a bright flash a moment before touching the sword so that he can easily avoid. He had similar experiences in China. A special day, a Chinese soldier shot and suddenly he was surprised not so excited to see him standing behind her, as soon as he pulled the trigger gun.

Shortly after the billions of applicants to the Navy officer, Ueshiba Morihei Patriarch back garden to the stream to wash. The main person at that time was enlightened. A sudden feeling that he can not be proactive and found myself suddenly become pure. At the same time, he began to feel heaven and earth shaking. From the ground like a golden iridescent light radiating, while touching his body, it can transform itself and radiate a majestic aura. He heard the bird call and found myself feeling the secrets of the creator.

Main at that time he understood the source of Budo was love and true spirit, is not true Budo opponent to win by force that keeps the peace of the world, feel and helps to develop all species, all things. He understood that the practice will lead people to that place of fullness, to the state of grace, in which people feel the harmony of the material world and spiritual world.

If the participation spirit exists in all Japanese martial arts are in fact never had someone to dig it includes the love of humanity as the true purpose of Budo Love is not jealous, love is not hate. That is why Ueshiba Morihei Patriarch decided to call his martial art is Aikido.

"Mon martial ideal": Aikido (the words of Patriarch Judo)

Since 1926, the name of Patriarch Morihei Ueshiba was known to many people and many famous martial art as well as national political figure, military are expected to visit him.

In 1927, at the invitation of Admiral Takeshita (12) Morihei Ueshiba Patriarch to Tokyo and started teaching for senior officers and the nobility. He also held special training classes for 21 days, the officers of the royal guard, but most were brought in at least five subjects offer Judo and Kendo.

He also taught at many other places in Tokyo. After that, he was Prince Shimazu for a large room for the dojo. Soon, the room became too cramped, and after many tries, he set up a dojo in Wakamatsu named Kobokan

It was here, one day the founder of the sect Judo - Jigoro Kano visited the Patriarch as he heard the name of his new sect. When looking Morihei Ueshiba Patriarch Aikido in the test development techniques on the pitch, master Jigoro Kano said: "This is the ideal martial." The next day, he sent

the disciples to Kobukan to learn Aikido.

At that time, hiring a strict disciple, explore our training very hard, to the point where it was known there as "hell on earth."

During the war years, the road only moderately active and is largely due Kisshomaru sensei Ueshiba (son of Patriarch) in charge of training. For his part, Patriarch Morihei Ueshiba at Iwama way back to Tokyo 120 km, where the temple now Aikido.

In 1946, the U.S. banned all martial arts training throughout Japan dojo in Tokyo and used as shelters for families of war victims. Until 1948, that office called Hombu Dojo (The director of the school). Aikido martial is first allowed to operate on land in the viscera by its spirit of reconciliation.

Dated 09/02/1948, Kobukai become Aikikai organization and recognition of education as a public meeting. Since then, the number of the students constantly increased, and some martial arts from Aikido today more inequality began to practice their work here. In the '50s, Patriarch Ueshiba Morihei - lost in her upcoming weeks - have been ceded back to work teaching children and the elevation of their charge. Among them, leaving many people go abroad and spread Aikido throughout the world.

When the Patriarch of the reconstituted on 26/04/1969 Hombu dojo is a large three-story buildings and Aikido are hundreds of thousands of people enrolled in the five continents.

Patriarch of four children, one girl and three boys. Two sons, early childhood loss and his son left is the direct successor to the Patriarch. Current leaders Center Aikido martial arts world is Moriteru Ueshiba (grandson Patriarch).

Since then, the Aikikai house was raised two stories and five classes outside regular exercise each day there are classes for the students or special groups. From 6 am to 8 pm, hundreds of people to practice at the dojo central path to the magic that Ueshiba Morihei Patriarch outlined.

Founder of General Motors

Not being a technical genius like Henry Ford or Daimler, William Crapo Durant but was on par with the giants in the world. He is the founder of General Motors, the group's biggest car makers now ...

William Crapo Durant was born in 1861 in Boston (USA) in a poor family. In the age of 16, after a tense debate with his principal, William Crapo Durant had voluntarily decided to stop going to school to earn money to support her and help her. Mother of William Crapo very sad to say but do not suggest son.

William Crapo Durant ready to do any job and proved to have special skills in business. First he sold firewood to receive rent for a cousin. Soon after, William Crapo switch pharmacies selling weed. More words found selling cigarettes, William Crapo Durant leave pharmacies to sell tobacco.

At 18, that William Crapo quick resourcefulness, the owner of a company trading in real estate has invited him to do. Here, William Crapo Durant also learn the accounting profession. He also picked up a lot of knowledge about financial and banking activities through selling their homes for insurance companies.
Also through the introduction of his real estate company owner, William Crapo Durant had made the company the production of clean water in Flint neighborhood. William Crapo Durant accountants for the company. Often are not new to the water companies are in crisis and in danger of bankruptcy. Be careful in key positions, great

ideas and determination of William Crapo Durant strong help the company escape. From the brink of bankruptcy, just two years after reform, water companies have become profitable.

From horse-drawn vehicles to automobiles.

Success with water supply companies that desire to make independent business man William Crapo Durant growing. Along with his friend Durant Dort, in 1886, William Crapo Durant was boldly borrowed $ 1,500 to buy a hybrid car factory horse. Durant-Dort Company Company was established and specialized in manufacturing wooden two-wheeled vehicles pulled by horses. Selling cars and William Crapo Durant more wealth.

Not stop at what has been achieved, he sought to invest with the assets acquired. But the failure involved a significant investment when the stock made him wake up. In 1905, how many assets, he dropped out to buy the production company of the Buick automobile engines, the owner cum designer motivated people of Scotland. Not enough $ 1.5 million, William Crapo Durant look to banks for loans. Just as his boss, just as director, William Crapo Durant directly operating on everything from project design, organization of production, advertising sales to financial management. His depth and detail to detail whether the company is growing with thousands of employees.

Founder of General Motors.

William Crapo Durant had many meetings and negotiations with Henry Ford and Ransom Olds, later known as the biggest competitors of General Motors. He again raised the investment capital of the bank and bought a series of small automotive equipment company, and merger and restructuring the department, the factory of Buick Motors.

In 1908, Buick Motor Company was renamed the General Motors Corporation, of which William Crapo Durant was a major shareholder and Chairman and CEO first. He has strength in its ability to manage, but not be able to design models such as Henry Ford. General Motors main stage is a secret new car models to compete, then William Crapo Durant was also right on with the idea is quite unique and unexpected. He asked his engineers when no new models to bring the oldest vehicles to fix some more to hit the market.

Oldtimes models of the first generation was William Crapo Durant boss asked to do a broader, longer than to sit comfortably, legs stretched out and be mass produced. The main line of Cadillac's luxury giant General Motors was born from the mouth of his command by President William Crapo Durant.

In 1911, under pressure from shareholders are banks, William Crapo Durant left the position of executive chairman of General Motors. But immediately, with the help of some capital investment, William Crapo Durant re-establish a new automobile manufacturing companies as Chevrolet Motors. Only three years after car manufacturing company of William Crapo Durant with interest, to the surprise and admiration of many. Chevrolet Motors' net profit in 1915 reached over $ 1.3 million, while General Motors is difficult and unprofitable. William Crapo Durant was on the red carpet as chairman and CEO of General Motors.

William Crapo Durant has made great contributions to General Motors contributed to capture significant market share and become a major automobile manufacturing corporation in the world of the future. After this no longer works for General Motors, he again set up car manufacturing company called Durant Motors family.

Founder Group and Apollo development.

For many people, the John Sperling beyond grim fate to become an intellectual, a successful entrepreneur has become a legend.

From a young boy had suffered too many disadvantages in life, John Sperling tried to become a teacher, then turned to business. In the heart of a passionate teacher, after extraordinary efforts, John Sperling founded the Apollo Group and University of Phoenix's reputation, environment and vocational training for those without jobs.

After more than 40 years of building thick, John Sperling has put Apollo Group and University of Phoenix before becoming a small institution of international stature. And John Sperling has become one of the world's richest man, owns the total assets of $ 1.5 billion individuals.

From concept research training program for an audience of people of working age in the John Sperling from the 70s of last century, the system of vocational education and training has been developed and are in the organization University of Phoenix and Apollo also founded by John Sperling.

Thanks to premium features Vietnam, Apollo and the University of Phoenix is constantly asserted the importance of education of society, has gradually expanded to many areas of training for many different audiences and reaching the world. Only in 2005, Apollo Group's total revenue reached 2251 billion figure to hundreds of large and small branches operating in the region in the world.

Childhood filled with hardship.

John Sperling had suffered a childhood full of hard, hard as in the fairy tales. He was born in 1921 in the Missouri Ozarks, United States, in a poor family with six siblings. John Sperling poor families to the whole house just to live in a small hut with a daily life lacks everything.

However, these difficulties for John Sperling has not seeped into first because from birth, John Sperling has endured the mother's authoritarianism, plus the frequent beatings of his father.

7, John Sperling was suffering from acute pneumonia and was bedridden for 6 months. The consequences of this disease is that many years later, when passed from John Sperling has always been exhausted, do legs shake and tremble, to say also stuttered. Until now, when my childhood thoughts to his misery, John Sperling had blurted out: "I did learn something in his childhood except that the sense of savings to be frugal escape difficult lives and go out to the outside world. "

Whether endured hard lives accumulating, not good health, even difficult reading, but John Sperling has not given up the will is determined in the study. Graduated from high school, because there is no money to study,

John Sperling has asked staff to do loading and unloading at a merchant ship crossing the sea route running between Shanghai and Japan, Panama and New York with a life not less arduous.

After two years of floating on the sea, with a small amount of money saved, John Sperling has decided to leave and go to school tuition at Oregon's Reed College in Portland. During the study, John Sperling would continue to work in the Columbia River shipyard and he totally does not have a string to make contact with family or any concept about the way the business later. John Sperling beginning at that time only a thought "study is the only way out for her existence."

Try to pass the Cambridge University, after years of hard work, learning to make money to feed their own self, and graduated from John Sperling has been accepted to the school's volunteer faculty of San Jose State University in State San Jose. Also at San Jose State University, he joined the Association of Teachers (AFT) and then by reputation, enthusiasm, and his talent, he was elected to the leadership position of the Association.

Work at San Jose State University, John Sperling has confirmed his talent in the field of teaching and student colleagues and respect. By 1972, John Sperling has decided to transfer the program to work for the organization of workshops for the police about crime problems of children adolescents ages.

Although very busy at work preparing and organizing the workshop agenda, but with passion and enthusiasm of a teacher, John Sperling has closely followed issues related to education. Facing unemployment and partly on a lot of reasons that cause the state law violations, John Sperling has an idea of research to develop a training program for people of working age to but never had the chance to be trained.

As a qualified teacher who spent many years working in environmental education, John Sperling has embarked on research, outlines specific training programs, the same time invited the former co-starred comments. Only a time not long after that, the program has been completed and put into practical application test.

It can be said right from the initial idea for the next step to try to apply, with positive implications for the community, the program was John Sperling people responded.

Successfully built the Apollo Group.

Special education program of John Sperling, after being put into application has quickly become the primary means to contribute to give the market a large volume of qualified workers, are trained.

To be able to apply their program effectively and more

broadly, John Sperling has links with the University of San Francisco to work together to expand training programs and ongoing profit gain success than expected wait. After taking into account the viability of this training model in a society there are many unemployed people, John Sperling has decided to collect the whole set up of capital should organize training for the Apollo and to profit in 1976 was University of Phoenix private school located in California.

As the calculations of John Sperling, in the first year enrollment, the number of people enrolled in the branches of Apollo and the University of Phoenix has reached more than 100.00 people. Fast on the rise rapidly, in the 80's, University of Phoenix has been recognized as the largest private university in the U.S. education system. Most recently, in 2006, the estimated number of people attending school has reached 280,000 people.

Over time, learning objects become more diverse, specialized knowledge about the increasingly expanding and require specialized, John Sperling has conducted the Apollo program expanded out in the region and beyond . John Sperling has invested large amounts of finance to improve facilities, hire more teachers are good subjects to work, thus, the Apollo has maintained training programs while expanding the traditional multiple areas such as computer science, mathematics, engineering, foreign language for all ages in the training level masters and doctoral specializations. Training content is continually added new, practical applications in the increasingly high.

In 1990, when the Internet on the rise rushing in the U.S. and other developed nations, John Sperling did not hesitate to spend large investments in purchasing equipment, technology, staff training and included in the application of the Apollo program. Through online training program leading prestige in the U.S., the number of students looking to enroll on an increase.

Through strategic step, John Sperling has also created many important base to expand training programs to many countries around the world such as Puerto Rico, Alberta, British Columbia, Netherlands, Mexico ... On average , the number of students enrolled in the high branches of Apollo annual increase of 25%.

By 2005, total income of the Apollo has grown to 2251 billion dollars. Apollo also officially ranked as one of the leading educational institutions the world and get the full name of Apollo Group.

Oriented business to benefit the community.

To be successful today, John Sperling and several times

had to bear the criticism and pressure because many people believe that he has used professional educators in business and making money, that's not the job accordance with professional ethics.

However, John Sperling said that the trading profits and there must be any lines of business which may, but more important issue is the first goal for the development of society. The main thought right that he constantly urged the business and dedication.

John Sperling has been invited to join the group on genetic research and the personal John Sperling has also contributed major funding for this research. Not only a leader in the charity, poor relief, to contribute ideas for programs of social reform in the country, John Sperling has spent huge finances for more than 10 million on the renovation project into sea water used in agriculture in poor countries in the region of West Africa bordering the sea to help the people in this area.

Is a well-known businessman, with a spirit of continuous learning progressive spiritual work tirelessly so you've turned 80, he had the hands of property giant $ 1.5 billion. Although rich and famous, John Sperling remains a simple man, hardworking and do not forget the habit up from 5 hours 30 am and work 12 hours a day.

Many people, including the leading intellectuals of the United States also had to admire and acknowledge that "beyond cruel fate with iron willpower and mental discipline, what did John Sperling is a rare event in the history of the business of mankind. "

Founder Benz cars and three-pointed star

Karl Friedrich Benz (11/25/1844 - 04/04/1929) is an engine manufacturer and a German automobile engineer. He has been recognized as the inventor of the automobile powered by gasoline engines. Two other German contemporaries, Gottlieb Daimler and Wilhelm Maybach, also independent studies on the same with his invention, but Benz was granted a patent for his work and then he was granted a patent for all both major components make up combustion engine.

In 1885, he built the Motorwagen, the first passenger cars equipped with gas engines. This car has three wheels, the steering wheel in the front passenger and the engine is mounted on two rear wheels (now a car so called tricycles). In addition, he also invented the carburetor, or speed system called accelerator, ignition system for spark from the battery, buzi ignition, clutch, gear and radiator cooling.
In 1896, Karl Benz designed and patented the first internal combustion engine with pistons horizontally in

opposite directions with each other. This is also the design principles of high performance engines used for sports cars.

Benz founded the Benz Company, precursor of Daimler-Benz, Mercedes-Benz and DaimlerChrysler. Before his death, he witnessed the explosion of demand for car use during the 1920s thanks to his invention.

Early.

Karl Benz (Karl Friedrich Michael Vaillant) was born in Karlsruhe, Germany. His father was a train driver named Johann George Benz and Josephine Vaillant mother. Moment he was born, they have not officially married, and must move into their new married in 1845. When Karl round two, his father died because of a rail accident, and his name was changed to Karl Friedrich Benz in remembrance to the father.

Although living in poverty, but his mother still tries to school his kindness. Benz School to study the local Grammar School at Karlsruhe and became an excellent student. In 1853, at 9 years old, he was in a school specializing in science Lyzeum. Then he entered the Polytechnic University under the direction of Ferdinand Redtenbacher.

Initial vocational training Benz locksmith, but eventually

followed his father's locomotive engineer training. 15 years old, he passed the exam to be a mechanical engineer and enrolled at the University of Karlsruhe. He graduated on 9/7/1864.

This time, when using bicycles, he began forming the concept of a car that later became wagon without a horse.

After finishing, Benz has 7 years of professional training in a few companies, but he did not see fit to any company. He started in Karlsruhe with two years doing different jobs at an engineering company. Then he moved to Mannheim to make a sketch and is a designer in a company draw ratio. In 1868, he went to Pforzheim work for construction companies to Gebruder Benckiser Eisenwerke und Maschinenfabrik, and then to Vienna for a short time working at a construction company and iron. Benz's Factory and the first inventor (1871-1882)

In the age of 27 (1871), with Karl Benz founded August Ritter in Mannheim plant mechanic (also aims to provide all construction materials): The mechanical and molding, then renamed the manufacturing plant sheet metal machinery.

In the first years of the plant is a dismal failure. Ritter no longer trusted the local authorities shall order confiscation of the factory. Benz bought out Ritter's shares in the company's dowry of his wife, fiancée,

Benz and Ringer married on 20.7.1872, had five children: Eugen (1873), Richard (1874), Clara (1877), Thilde (1882), and Ellen (1890).

Because the business is not so lucky Karl Benz move to develop new engines. To get more revenue, in 1878, he began to make the new patent. At first, he concentrated all efforts to create a second term gas engines are reliable, based on 4-stroke engine designs by Nikolaus Otto. Benz finished his engine on New Year's Eve and was patented in 1879.

Karl Benz showed his real talent through continuous innovation, while making two-stroke engine. He was granted a patent for the speed system, ignition system for battery ignition, buzi ignition, carburetor, clutch, gear and radiator coolant.

Fabrik Company Gasmotoren-Benz's Mannheim (1882-1883)
The issue arose again when the bank merger requests in Mannheim Gas Company of Benz because it maintains the high production costs. Benz was forced to rescue by linking with photographer Emil Buhler and his brother (a cheese merchant) to get the support of the bank. The company became joint-stock company Gasmotoren Fabrik Mannheim in 1882.
After all necessary agreements, Benz dissatisfied because he only left 5% of the shares and a modest position as director of the company. Worse , his ideas are not paying attention to when designing new products, so

he withdrew from the partnership only a year later (1883).

Benz & Cie. and the Motorwagen

Lifelong passion Benz has taken him to a bicycle repair shop of Max Rose and Friedrich Wilhelm Esslinger. In 1883, the three formed a new company producing industrial machines called Benz & Company Rheinische Gasmotoren-Fabrik, also called Benz & Cie.. Rapid growth with 25 employees, the company would soon embark on the production of gas engines.

The company gave Benz the opportunity to meet the desired design is not a horse wagon. Based on the experience and love bike, he has used similar technology to create a car using 4-stroke engines of his own place between the two rear wheels. Chain capacity is transmitted through gears to the rear axle. Benz finished his invention in 1885 and named it the Benz Patent Motorwagen. It was the first car designed whole, not simply a motorized rickshaw. So, Karl Benz is considered the inventor of the automobile.
The beginning of Motorwagen in 1885 was not as expected. The tests often attracted many viewers. They laughed sarcastically when the vehicle crashed into a wall because it initially difficult to control. The

Motorwagen be patented DRP-37435 on 29/02/1886: "gas-powered vehicles." The first successful test was conducted in early summer in 1886 on public roads. The following year, Karl Benz created the Motorwagen Model 2 with a few changes, and in 1887, Model 3 with wooden wheels debut.

Benz began selling cars - under the name Ad-Benz Patent Motorwagen Motorwagen and became the first car to be put into the market. Customer First (late summer 1888) is a person working in a mental hospital. Buyers Monday, Emile Roger, a Paris, has a profound influence the success of the Benz. In a period of several years, Roger has been producing Benz engines under license by him, and in 1888, decided to add his car into production line. So a lot of Benz cars manufactured in France and sold by Roger, because at that time, who seem very fond of Paris by car.

The first customer facing many serious problems. Meantime, gasoline is only available in pharmacies and is sold as a cleaning product, and not stored in large quantities. Moreover, in 1888 the first version of the Motorwagen to push when going uphill. This restriction was overcome after Berta Benz made her famous trip, drive one car go a far distance and suggested her husband added a different gear. Famous story came from a morning of 5/8/1888, Berta Benz took the car of Benz (her husband did not know this), and made the long walk 106 kilometers from Mannheim to Pforzheim to visit her mother, carrying her two sons Eugen and Richard.

Besides having managed to get petrol as fuel in the pharmacy on the way, she must overcome many technical problems and finally arrived at the sky grow dark Pforzheim, announced his achievement to Karl Benz by telegram. Today, the event was held in Germany in a stock car race.

Benz Model 3's debut around the world in 1889 world fair in Paris, and about 25 Motorwagen produced in the period between 1886 and 1893.

Scaling Benz & Cie.

As the demand for internal combustion engines still growing, Benz was forced to expand the factory, and in 1886 he added a new building located in Waldhofstrasse (active until 1908). Benz & Cie.. developed during the transition from 50 workers (1890) to 140 (1899). During the late 19th century - Benz & Company - is the largest car company in the world with 572 cars produced in 1899.

In 1899, Benz & Cie. become joint stock companies with participation of Friedrich Von Fischer and Julius Ganss, two foreigners are members of the board. Ganss working at the Chamber of Commerce.

The new director should recommend Karl producing less expensive vehicles to suit a range of production requirements. In 1893, Benz built the Victoria, a two-seat car with a 3HP motor, can reach speeds of 11mph, and a front axle is operated by a key driving force in roller wheel for navigation. This model was successful with 45 units sold in 1893.

One year later (1894) Benz improved this design in his new Velo model. This car was produced on a large scale - from 1894 to 1200 a 1901 - to the extent it is considered the automobile was first mass-produced. Benz Velo also participated in the first automobile race Paris to Rouen 1894

In 1895, Benz built the first truck in history. Some aircraft are then Netphener bus company, bus company first in history, changed little.

Karl Benz was granted a patent for boxer engine with pistons horizontally in opposite directions in 1896. The corresponding pistons simultaneously touching dead, so that will balance each other about momentum. Flat 4 engine or some kind of engine cylinder boxer is the most common and is called reverse horizontal piston engine. This is the principle design of the engine high performance race cars such as Porsches.

Although Daimler died in 03/1900, and there is no evidence to suggest Karl Benz and Gottlieb Daimler know each other as well known achievements of each other first, but the competition with Daimler Motors (DMG) in Stuttgart has began challenging leaders of Benz & Cie. 10/1900 on the DMG main designer, Wilhelm Maybach, has introduced the Mercedes-35HP at the request of Emil Jellinek in the contract. Jellinek purchased 36 units, and he became a dearler of this model. Although Maybach left DMG in 1907, but he is the designer of this model and all of its important changes. After testing, the first car was delivered to Jellinek on 22/12/1900. Jellinek proposed changes continue to model and obtained good results in the following years, promoting DMG increase production of this car model.

Counterattack by the Parsifil Benz, released in 1903, with two-cylinder and a maximum speed of 37mph. Then, the other directors had hired some French designers without the advice of the Benz. (France is a country with developed auto industry based on Maybach's invention.) Because of this move, after intense discussions, on 24/02/1903, Karl Benz decided to retire, not management design more reasonable, although he remains a director of the board until losing in 1929. Two sons Eugen and Richard Benz is also leaving the company, but Richard returned in 1904 in his capacity as an automotive designer guests.

Until 1904, sales of Benz & Cie.da 3480 increased the company and the company remains the leading automobile manufacturers. Although still involved in the board of Benz & Cie., But Karl Benz soon find yourself another company and working with his son, Eugen. The company has close relationships with his family, manufacturing automobiles under a different brand.

In 1909, Benz & Cie. production and the Blitzen Benz racing car has set a record speed of 288.1 km / h, is considered a "faster than any aircraft, train or automobile that" at that time. It maintains a record of this in the next 5 years.

Benz-Söhne (1906 - 1923)

Karl Benz and his son, Eugen, moved to Ladenburg, and with its own capital, they founded Sons Benz (Benz-Söhne) in 1906, automobile production and gas engines. Gas engine was later replaced by a gasoline engine due to lack of demand.

Benz-Söhne Cars of good quality and become more common as taxis in London. In 1912, Karl Benz liquidation of all shares in the Benz-Söhne and leave the company to Eugen and Richard. In his 70-year-old round (25/11/1914), Karl Benz was awarded the University of Karlsruhe University PhD.

Almost from the beginning of the automobile industry, the presence of sports car racing has become a way to promote brands. Initially, the model production speed racing participation and presence in the Benz Velo was the first automobile race Paris to Rouen 1894. Then, the investment for the development of racing sports cars bring more revenue from the automotive domain associated with the winner. The car racing is one of a kind produced at that time (which we can see in the image of the Benz), motor vehicle and the aerodynamics are designed first, Tropfenwagen, was about presented at the European Grand Prix 1923

350 cars were produced in 1923, last year the company Benz-Shone. In the following year, 1924, Karl Benz produced two additional 8 / 25 hp for the purposes of his own, so he never sold them. Currently, two cars are still preserved.

Towards Daimler-Benz and Mercedes Benz (1926) During the First World War, both Benz & Cie. and Daimler Motors (DMG) will increase production of large quantities of war service. After the war ended, both manufacturers back to normal activities, but the German economy, which were severely assaulted. Cars are considered luxury items and are taxed at 15%. At the same time, Germany was in a severe gasoline shortage. To cope with this difficulty, in 1919, at the suggestion of Karl Benz, Benz & Cie. DMG proposal through cooperation with representatives Karl Jahn, but DMG refused this offer.

The economic crisis in Germany is becoming worse. In 1923, Benz & Cie. only 1328 units produced in Mannheim, and the DMG 1020 in Stuttgart. The average price of a car is 25 million marks by rapid inflation. The two companies return to negotiations and in 1924 signed an agreement of mutual benefits take effect until 2000. Both firms have the same standardized design, production, purchase, sale and advertising-market automotive products and their - though still holding its own label.

Finally, Benz & Cie. on 28/07/1926. and DMG merged into Daimler-Benz and the company named its cars are Mercedes Benz honoring the most important model of the DMG, Mercedes-35HP. DMG model name is selected by the name of her 10-year-old Mercedes Jellinek daughter of Emil Jellinek (as it is one of the partners of the DMG), who has set the technical standards for new models. A new logo was created-including three-pointed star (representing Daimler's motto: "engines for road, waterway and air routes") is surrounded by laurel branches of traditional logo Benz - and are labeled Mercedes-Benz. The next year (1927), the number of cars sold at triple the 7918 and diesel used for truck production. In 1928, Mercedes Benz SS unveiled.

On 04/04/1929, Karl Benz passed away at his home in Ladenburg at the age of 84 due to bronchial inflammation.

Frederick W. Smith - The founder of Federal Express cargo

Today, Federal Express Company, also referred to as FedEx, have no stranger to the United States population, or said that for the wider world. Today, the delivery of FedEx boxes were found placed everywhere, businesses and ordinary people are accustomed to fast delivery services of FedEx and every day do not know how many companies, trust lost connections, canceled a lease sale, has been rescued in time due to the existence of Federal Express.

But about 30 years ago, when Frederick W. Smith, the founder of Federal Express Company, a new opinion in an essay submitted while attending Yale, he was professor of criticism as "utopia."

Frederick W. Smith was born into a wealthy family in Memphis, Tenessee. His father passed away when he was 4 years old should be about childhood he had to rely on the guidance of the uncles, and especially from the teachers at school. Smith said that two people have the most effect on him when they entered high school English teacher is a teacher and gymnastics coach. English teacher pointed out to him that this world has many things he can learn, including those from people who have lived before him hundreds of thousands of years so he could apply to life. Master fitness trainer training for his spirit always try, do not be discouraged despite failure to first. Growing up, as in life, Federick W. Smith carry the instructions and he said that this is what contributed greatly to his success.

During the study at Yale University, Frederick W. Smith soon realized the world around you will change very much for the computer industry has advanced so quickly and are increasingly more applications in society. He wrote an essay in a class of trade, said the need to change the way enterprises operate, especially about the distribution and movement of goods so that we can meet the demands of a social Assembly automation and computerization. The year was 1966, his professor did not agree on what he referred to criticism, as "utopia" and the low point.

Graduated from college, he volunteered to join the Marines and was sent to Vietnam during the war to the most exciting period. The rich, letters of students leaving school have been thrown into the battlefield, he was trying hard to adapt to new circumstances. Fred Smith said that he remembered from the old Standing upper PhD, senior military service for many years as "just lieutenant to remember three things: fire, when necessary, continuous move and ordered us to clear".

In the army, he was only gradually realized what I wrote in the essay while in school are true. The idea of Federal Express is the company formed from it.

Military where a lot of waste. On both human lives and goods supplies. Supplies to be moved out front and a massive indiscriminate, given to places no demand, while most places need not be. Ideas do have a distribution

After two round of war in Vietnam and after more than four years in the army, Frederick W. Smith retired, returned to civilian life. In a later interview, he said "I want to do something with character building after blowing up too many things on the battlefield."

He went to borrow, to persuade relatives to put funds together, and with the amount of 80 million Federal Express Company, also known as FedEx, was formed in 1971. His service began modestly, only delivered a small kit and paper documents. In the first night began operations, including a fleet of 14 jet aircraft took off with only 186 packages only.

The market has not grown as fast as he wanted. Overnight delivery is an urgent need at that time because no one knew to ask. In the first two years of operation, the company suffered losses of 27 million dollars. In just a short time, his company at risk of default. Around that Frederick W. Smith has dissipated the investors' capital, as well as his contribution to his sister and relatives in the house. But Mr. Smith does not rot, he negotiated with the bank moratorium and eventually attract enough bargain to help the company survive.

Unlike many other investors, Frederick W. Smith is also a talented chief executive. From the very beginning, he was aware that information is the key factor to help companies succeed as well as transcends all other competitors. Information on place of origin of goods, is where will go, will never come, how much money prices, bills sent to anyone ... all equally important to the delivery

One other basics that he wanted his employees to really feel that they have a direct impact to the success of the company. The executives of the company are thoroughly trained to ensure the respect of our employees and have been under the necessity of understanding between the employer and the employee. Fred Smith believes that fair treatment would lead to staff loyalty and company loyalty is always to help companies overcome all difficulties.

Indeed, to come in 1997, FedEx has the company worth around 16 billion dollars, with 170,000 employees, fleet of 584 aircraft and 38.500 full range of transport vehicles to transport and distribution 2.8 million packages per day in 212 countries. In that year, FedEx has the opportunity to demonstrate their capabilities to customers. That strikes at UPS (United Parcel Service), FedEx rival companies. Overnight, the FedEx office to receive 800,000 additional packages each day. But thousands of FedEx employees, many who have worked all day, have volunteered to work overtime on the previous night to help select filter, distribution of packages. Mr. Smith's effort to thank their employees through word of thanks posted on the 11-page national newspaper as well as cash reward for employees.

When the UPS strike ended, many customers have not returned to the company that signed a permanent contract with FedEx and increase market share of the company to add two more points, to nearly 45%.

But Fred Smith did not fall asleep on the win. Continue to

improve as one of the basics of operating his opinion. FedEx add public computer systems at the office of more than 100,000 customers and data traffic for its own needs for nearly 700,000 more customers. The result is about 60% of FedEx customers can print labels on the containers to be sent. FedEx received information from the customer to pick up goods, transport and delivery. FedEx's rivals are still struggling to keep up the chase for the advancement of their technology.

Professor Fred Smith at Yale can not overlook the importance of ideas to help entrepreneurs worldwide to and taken quickly, overnight, but now this is what the Company indispensable. For the purpose of reducing operating costs and have to avoid excessive inventories of goods, companies today are applying the method of "just in time", it should be found to where to put it to storage, not so much , has recently ease capital shortage problem? products become obsolete. And as such it needs a shipping company like FedEx increasingly important.

The outbreak of the internet and the development of the global economy also contributed to the growth of the company FedEx. With the new facilities in the Philippines and Taiwan, the road transport system and particularly in mainland China, FedEx is in position ready to meet the new demands of the world.

And perhaps the world will continue to develop the

student as to what Frederick W. Smith predicted the essay submitted in class more than 30 years ago.

The founder of the Red Cross

Where he himself to misery of humankind, the shadow flag red cross on a white background as a contribution to pure hands to alleviate the pain. War, natural disasters, epidemics, heavier .. will not be the consequence of the hands of humanism, the community contributes to overcome.

In 1901, Nobel Peace Prize was awarded to two of the Henry Dunant and Frédéric Passy. Frédéric Passy which has asked the leaders of international peace movement. Henry Dunant was also the father of the Red Cross.

WAR IN THE NORTH UNIVERSITY FOOTBALL ITALIA.

Henry Dunant, the Swiss president of joint-stock company specialized in the production of a water mill in Algeria. But in his hand is not a license to use the waterfall in the colony as a source of motivation for the mill. So he went to Italy to find swimming in the third Napoleon to ask for the signature of the emperor. But on that fateful day 24-6-1859, Napoleon III was to command a battle at Solferino (Italy) between inter-France-Italy, while the other is the imperial Austro by Francois Joseph commanded 50,000 troops in Italy and 100,000 French troops fought fierce Austria with 160,000 men.

Maybe it was one of the bloodiest battles in human history. After more than a day together more than 40,000 population was eliminated from the round of fighting. Sprawl battle cries of the fallen and, groan cries of the wounded.

Witnessed the fall landscape, and blood flow found

wounded Union wagon on the churches, warehouses, houses are being requisitioned as a place to cure. Henry Dunant as has become a different person. He gathered people of good will, volunteer ambulance into a team dedicated to serve all regardless of which side wounded. This time the French, Austria or Italy are all human beings are in need of hand pain kindness. Catiglione towns where rescue wounded soldiers, has launched the slogan that would later affect humanitarian work around the world: "Tutti fratelli-All are brothers."

ROLL TO BOOK FOR LIFE.

Memoir he wrote about this war, was published in May Memmory 10-1862 titled A Memory of Solferino-of Solferino. These aspects of political, military aside. What he emphasized was horrible and unimaginable brutality of war emerged. The young boy was coated bullets at the end of the stones used to fight other people do not like their weapons. They rip through, rake structure like wild animals, cursing each other with all sorts of languages. These strangers plunge into barbarism, bloodshed by order of the kings with the consequences: "The French, German, Slavic, Arab, all located in a crowded synagogue .. This is a soldier face completely disfigured, his tongue sticking out his jaw broken. He wants to move and sit up. I dipped a washcloth in a bucket of water and then squeeze the water flowing into the crater that is mouth before ... "

The conclusion of his memoir, he made a call to the world: Each country should organize a charity to happen during the war, could help the wounded, irrespective of national citizenship. This book was sent to several characters of power and political influence at the time. Readers around the world were shocked and agreed with his opinion.

ESTABLISHMENT Red Cross.

. Gustave Moynier, president of the public welfare, together with Geneva and several other characters Dunant founded the International Committee of the relief of the injured. It is the forerunner of the Red Cross today. Actually, the president of this committee is Dufour, Henry Dunant as secretary. The three remaining members are Moynier and 2 MD is the Appia and Maunoir.

In 1863, the Committee invited representatives of major powers to meet in Geneva, with 36 delegates from 14 European countries. The conference began on day 26-10

- When the soldiers removed from combat round, even when they do not take action to resist, they will not be treated as violent. Health care providers, regardless of faction will fight hard to help them.
- The military medical staff or volunteers of the charity will never be attacked. But they are also not allowed to carry weapons. To distinguish in the field, they are allowed to carry a separate sign on your arm. Tribute to Switzerland, home of the Red Cross, a sign that the red cross on a white background (the Swiss flag is a white cross on red background).

Date 8-8-1864 at Geneva, 24 members from 16 European countries sent to the same few U.S. observers to attend the conference through this first convention. The U.S. envoy had presented the Committee's experience in sanitation and health care of their country in the ongoing war (1861-1865). They say, voluntary organizations have operated very effectively, how to work the consent of the government close to what Henry Dunant proposed. The first Convention of the Red Cross was adopted, the following conventions are also many modifications sung.Rieng U.S. until 1882, then officially joined the Red Cross.

Today, all states and territories have signed the convention and forced to humane treatment of wounded soldiers, prisoners of war and must be protected form of civilian victims of war ... Committee Meeting International Red Cross based in Geneva, made the task of monitoring respect for conventions.

LIFE SECTION sad but happy ending.

Humanitarian work by the Henry Dunant succeeded beyond expected. But his business is the opposite. Too focused on the activities of the Red Cross, he had no time for many companies. By 1867, his company went bankrupt. He also resigned as member of the Red Cross, to leave Geneva. Do not have a stable job, no support from friends, hang out place to find a livelihood elsewhere, there are times when giving money to live in the galaxy ... He was then residing in a house the small village of Heiden, Switzerland. Here, some new acquaintances who have contaminated water and introduced him to a chore in the local hospital for 18 years.

A young Swiss journalist accidentally find out the whereabouts of Henry Dunant in 1895, requested permission to interview. After the article was published, the individuals, organizations and governments in Europe have done much for his sponsors. Russian queen gave him a lifetime pension, many countries issuing coins, medals printed Dunant. In 1901, Henry Dunant Frédéric Passy, along with Nobel Peace Prize was awarded first.

His escape poverty, hard times, but he has long money and are no longer mean anything anymore. He donated all the money they have for charity. Rest of his life in a frugal, simple in a nursing home. Dated 30-10-1910 he quietly died in Heiden and funerals are held simply for his intentions.

Yahoo, building a strategic vision for success

Yahoo, the search engine on the Internet and at the same time as one of the largest media companies in the world there has been great development in the early years of last century, to become formidable opponents for many firms such as Google, or Microsoft's Hotmail.

Dubbed as "solid as stone table," Yahoo has demonstrated the success of its market information technology world.

With a strategic vision of their excellent, Yahoo deserves the success it is today. Yahoo's profit in the three months of 2004 doubled over the same period last year, reaching

The elements for building a strategic vision that Yahoo's excellent idea to develop proper and accurate perspective on the future.
*) The idea of developing the right:

Yahoo has bought Kelkoo company for $ 576 million initiative to expand online business Intenet. Thus, Kelkoo will become a subsidiary of Yahoo. All activities will Kelkoo by Yahoo board and driver control. This is a strategic step to expand Yahoo's e-commerce market potential, but has not been fully exploited.

Only in America, e-commerce reached $ 117 billion figure in the past 4 years. In Europe, online shopping and spending to 48.5 billion dollars in 2004 alone and is forecast to reach 202.3 billion dollar figure in 2009.

Kelkoo is a company selling goods through the giant network in Europe, accounting for 10% of the market leader in the continent. Highlights of Kelkoo is the ability to compare prices. Through Kelkoo's search engine, customers can compare the prices of more than 2500 companies, 3 million products in 25 topics including books, movies, music, electronics, clothing ...

Pierre Chappaz, Kelkoo CEO said: "We believe that the combination of goods and services of Kelkoo to compare and global trading regime Yahoo will help us become a leading company in the sector and make online purchases. "

Pages traditional online advertising and search engine Yahoo has pushed profits higher. There's the search engine Yahoo was able to "comparable" with Google and more and more users.

As assessed by experts, site Yahoo.com is the most visited in the world and has been providing services such as private advertisements, but users must pay a fee.

The value of shares of Yahoo and other Internet companies have developed high return of market confidence, opening up a future for this market development. This means firms will have more opportunities to improve their profit, but to require that each firm must develop their own strategies to develop properly.

Along with the increased price of Yahoo shares and some other airlines, Nasdag technology index also increased. This is a sign for the growth of Internet companies as investors regained their confidence.

*) The vision of the future - The market for high-tech companies recover.

Previously, investors have shunned the Internet company called dot.com companies amid rumors that no one else for that companies will survive and be profitable . The main failure mass of dot.com companies was in for large companies operating in this area, such as NBC Internet

However, Yahoo remained firm stance that will not defeat this threat. Companies such as Yahoo even benefit from the fallout because advertisers like the Web site does have a crowded counter.

Through such strategic perspective, Yahoo has gone from success to continue this success on the market of information technology world.

Swatch, the symbol of the successful Swiss watch

Hundreds of the year, Swiss watch brand has become a symbol of quality worldwide. However, starting from 1970, along with the introduction of the industry watches Japan, USA, Germany ... Swiss watches were attacked violently.

Even the famous brands such as Rolex, Omega, Longhi also beaten ragged, sales plummeted. According to statistics, in 1985, the world produced about 440 million watches, Japan produced 170 million units accounting for 39% of total world production, a world leader. Hong Kong is 95 million units, accounting for 22% of total world production. That year, the manufacturer of Swiss watches are left with 286, thousands of workers from 10 down to just 8 thousand.

In the situation of the brand of quartz watches and clocks as Sieko Electric, Casio, ... tend to dominate the global reputation "Kingdom of the clock," the Swiss began slowdown. Clock industry has long been the pillar of the Swiss economy, second only to industrial and chemical engineering - the annual output value of nearly $ 3.1 billion. This change makes the Swiss watch industry to the hundreds of thousands of designs to find ways to cope, trying to back up and hope the new factors. And the magic came with the advent of the Swatch, one of the Swiss watch brand known today.

Since its establishment, Swatch has attracted the attention of the world with new structures and strong marketing style, quickly won the affection of numerous customers around the world. Only in the last 18 years, Swatch has sold over 300 million units world and Swatch watches have become a new phenomenon, a success unprecedented in the industry producing the clock.

Maker of Swatch watches is the largest in Switzerland, located in the Corporation includes 16 companies manufacturing watches such as Omega, Tissot, Longines, Rado, Hamilton, Blancpain, Breguet ... Swatch can say is the harmonious integration between manufacturing technology renowned Swiss watch with fashion and sports. Many customers commented:

The reason, Swatch brand has been successful as of today is thanks to the third step in the right:

1. Remove old replacement.

Swatch watches, in addition to forming a new design and innovation, the company has used plastic instead of stainless steel to make clock cases. Plastic coating applied modern techniques, clock cases plated yellow, silver, glistening ball really hard to distinguish fake. Changed so that the thickness and weight of the clock reduced, become beautiful, cost is also reduced significantly. Also, the battery can be replaced, just re-run exactly the trauma room, water-resistant.

2. Reasonable price.

Swatch said that the reason these kinds of quartz clocks and watches of Japanese and U.S. electronics quickly gain market mainly due to price, found nice. The correct target point, Swatch watches, through sophisticated processing, reducing materials, technical reform, which significantly reduced cost. Firms apply strategies to achieve a slim profit and market reputation, the unit price was around 25-35 dollars, thus enhancing the competitive ability compared to quartz watches from Japan. Many customers use the clock before the Japanese arrived, now with Swiss watches. Only in the U.S. market each year Swatch has sold over a million units.

3. Delicate policy consumption.

Customers today have the mentality that stores are selling the product surface so good clock. Recognizing this, Swatch sold only in large companies and clock shop class, building the image in the eyes of customers so trustworthy appearance, prices are lower than other types of watches made famous guests Swatch goods feel cheap, pretty good and hence consumption also increased the clock.

Today, the Swatch brand can be found in all subjects from pupils, students and staff to politicians, business people and those famous beautiful talent in the world. "Swatch is a symbol of success. Swatch is a fresh, young and also the pride of the people playing the famous clock - Swiss watch. "

Successes and failures of Nokia

If in the 90s of last century, cell phone maker Nokia of Finland is considered to be prosperity in Europe, only a decade later, its business has become "bi tick "the most. This major success or failure of Nokia are helping Europe to draw valuable lessons.

The emergence of Nokia in the field of mobile phone production in the 90 is to demonstrate the typical European competition foothold in the technology sector worldwide. Since its inception, Nokia mobile phones have built a powerful brand, quickly dominate the mobile market in most countries around the world. In the eyes of the world, the rise of Nokia as a symbol of European prosperity XXI century. In a speech in 2002, European Commission President Romano Prodi at the time was to emphasize the success of Nokia and rival Ericsson AB (Sweden) showed that Europe's capacity in research, development and high-tech applications.

However, because of "sleeping in the victory" and not subject to renewal, Nokia should have made serious mistakes. In three years, revenue and reputation of the company have fallen sharply, especially as Apple Inc. U.S. launch of smart phones iPhone in January 2007, Nokia's shares have fallen 47%. In a ranking of food brands in the world he created in 2010 by market research firm Brown Optimor Millwrard implementation, Nokia has dropped to 30th grade, dropped to No. 43. Although still accounting for one third of global phone sales, but seems like Nokia are now trapped. Recent studies show that while electronics manufacturers in Korea - including Samsung Electronics Co.. - Leading the market, then Apple's iPhone and Research In Motion Ltd.

BlackBerry dominates the high-level smartphone.

According to analysts, the very conservative business policy as well as complacency, not innovation, not affiliated with other companies operating in the field of information technology has made reputation, turnover, profits, shares of Nokia ... decline.

To avoid sliding into the Nokia car wound down, the European companies need to draw the following lessons:

- A Nokia is rapidly climbing the pinnacle of success, but soon satisfied with their accomplishments, only attention to the stock market without investing in research to bring new products to meet the tastes customer.

- Secondly, Nokia has been too loyal to the phone model is purely functional hearing, called, should have ignored the basic needs of our customers' time @ "which is check email, find fun places , entertainment and participate in networking sites like Twitter, Facebook.

- Three is the Nokia did not cooperate for mutual development with other companies in the industry. The building is a powerful brand in Finland Nokia has neglected to link to the website, the manufacturers of electronic devices. Nokia has forgotten the idea of innovation.

Perhaps the opportunity to fix mistakes, Nokia's reverse the situation has become tenuous, but Europe is still very much the leading company operating in key sectors of the economy such as oil , aircraft, pharmaceuticals, automotive and financial services.Europe needs to spend more time analyzing and evaluating the successes and failures of Nokia. Thus Europe can strengthen its position in the international arena.

Sennheiser's road to success

Headset company is world famous establishment in 1930, the real success in the years 70, 80 and known to this day.

Last April, organized the Association of American consumer electronics has honored him Professor Fritz Sennheiser to the great house (Consumer Electronics Hall of Fame). 95-year-old man who had founded the formidable brand name Sennheiser Electronic.

In early 1930 Fritz Sennheiser young man abandoned his initial ambition of the gardener to become a professional electronic engineer at the Technical Institute Heinrich-Hertz, Berlin (Germany). In the context of economic stagnation in Germany after the Second World War there is no opportunity for people like he studied and worked in the field of transmission of encrypted information, so he decided to set up business called :

Laboratory Wennebostel (Labor W). Siemens then acquired the entire product measurements of Labor W, accompanied by its own production order products MD1 microphone, a step in the production of micro village.

The '50s, when the market has known through Labor W & MD1 MD2 Micro products, the company emerged as a new equipment manufacturer prestigious studio, representing Germany. In 1950, manufacturing Labor W "micro invisible MD 3 (" invisible "mic), the product is little different from the first generation ago when it did not cover all aspects of performance. However, the most prominent product must include a professional microphone for MD 21 reporters. It first appeared in 1954 with durability, quality recording fidelity. This product is not the best selling (best seller), but also television, radio popular use in a long time afterwards.

Communications technology development leads to the strong expansion of the Labor W, revenue increased from half a million to 10 million mark German mark, workers from 67 people to 695 people. In 1858, while Labor W renamed Sennheiser Electronic, popular brands for today.

Into the 60s, Sennheiser product research and development is known as "open headphones" ("open" headphones) that previous products could not stand comparison: HD 414. Ultra-lightweight structure, the membrane wall to your ears by gently sucking thin film instead of using paper should sound very good, HD 414 students from the research as well as its long experience. That is why the Sennheiser factory capacity to 10 million HD 414, the best selling of all time.

MD 421 microphone studio sibling rival HD 414 also equally successful. 421 MD type microphones capture audio recording waves towards the heart (super-cardioid), it records the audio level from side to side 900 and a little behind the song spread. Fritz Sennheiser to create mechanisms for engineers creative freedom (freedom to play) goes against a request from the former sales team asked him to focus more on business. He spends up to 11% of total revenue for the study of optimization steps create momentum product competition, a strong jump in the consumer electronics market is booming.

In later years, when the Japanese manufacturer emerged strong with cheap products, the company Sennheiser decided to focus on the development of high quality products for customer oriented professional. This means that profits will be greater than that of ordinary consumer goods.

The late 70's, Sennheiser's distribution system has covered all of Europe, Asia and North America. They also noted that Soviet leaders during the Cold War also use

In 1982 marked a turning point in the history of the company, Fritz Sennheiser transferred management to his son Jörg Sennheiser, who decided to open the second development on the fields of electronics and mass market professionals.

Products highlighted in this decade is the system headset, microphone wireless technology uses infrared waves used in the largest station in Germany or outdoor concerts. Sennheiser headphones with noise canceling technology reputation NoiseGuard "Lufthansa is equipping its pilots. Reference microphone MKH 816 award-winning "Scientific and Engineering Award" awarded by the Academy of Sciences of the American motion picture, such as the Oscar awards in this field.

In 1992, Sennheiser microphone manufacturer repurchase senior Georg Neumann GmbH (founded 1928). In 2000, Sennheiser introduced the sound beam technology "Audio Beam" widely used in products company in the park sound system, exhibition, in the PC ...

Audio Beam technology based on principles of sound processing to focus sound waves similar to the principle of convergence of light beams. For instance in an exhibition area, other than the usual system of negative spillover vocalize all positions, Audio Beam generated towards the sound and located right in front of people stood listening only.

Sennheiser is expanding its subsidiaries in multiple countries like France, Britain, Belgium, Netherlands, Singapore, USA, Canada, Mexico and a joint venture with Danish William Demant Holding Company A / S of Denmark in 2003 formed powerful force.

PayPal - the amazing success of P2P payment models

Even in the early stages of the dot-com movement, when people insist that the Internet would revolutionize the publishing industry, broadcasting or retailers, the primary benefits of World Wide Web is to link individual people together.

Although many companies and investors adventure that will occupy the position of Internet journalism, television or shopping centers of the world's largest, in fact, this environment can almost phone only ... The most successful applications on the Internet (electronic mail, chating, broker ...) are not large corporations to help pass information to everyone who is helping individuals to

Companies such as eBay, Match.com, Classmates Online has overcome the period of decline of dot-com movement because they have to understand first of all Internet communication environment between man and man. They create favorable conditions to help people relate to each other. In a series of P2P services, is a company that has created a unique success by creating facilities for both ordinary people can do on the network that most people outside the network are implemented: the payment purchase goods or services.

But the simple miracle of the PayPal service is provided to allow two people to exchange money almost directly, in a way very secure and anonymous. It is not just the opening for an economy with individual personal style online, but also to explore a new way for merchants and small businesses who are not able to set up a trade account costly trade with major credit card companies.

EBay bought PayPal in 2002 for $ 1.5 billion, an act considered a "natural marriage" of two men of power in the P2P service. More than 60% of PayPal's business is the payment of the purchase in Ebay auction markets. Statistics of PayPal is an astonishing proof of the power of P2P network model. By the end of June 2003, the company has more than 31 million users, compared with about 27 million of the previous three months, and the transaction amount up to $ 2.8 billion in the first quarter, equivalent to 360 per second. Although some financial services companies like Citibank's C2it services, or even AOL have launched the P2P payment solution, but

PayPal has succeeded beyond most competitors.
With mainstream users, PayPal is because it replaces
the utility to go to the bank. Basic technology transfers
actually very simple. To make payments of Ebay, which
is the main activity of PayPal, only two pages of data
associated with very little exchange. Pay Now button on
the auction site to buy the goods will lead to a declaration
form which contains information about sales and
merchandise. Only in the final stage, if required to pay,
the new buyer is redirected to PayPal, which eBay has
attached information about the seller's certificate,
identification and description of other goods.
PayPal helps small businesses unable to open
commercial accounts with large credit card companies a
new means to accept online payments
One of the attractions of the PayPal payment is
anonymous: a buyer can pay for a lot of people and
different companies without having to send credit card
numbers or personal information to anyone outside
PayPal. "The ability to provide payment system safety
and anonymity of PayPal is a secret," Chief Technology
Officer Chuck Geiger said, "When you pay, I do not know
how he paid me. I just know that my account has
reported. "
Technology support behind (back-end) to handle money
transfers nearly networks based on the availability of
credit card companies and banking transactions.
Transactions with banks, PayPal also use the network
inter-bank payment as most banks use the system and
the basics of credit card payment by credit card
associations set. Mr. Geiger said, "The trick is to take

advantage of PayPal's most practical technology, which users are attracted by the comprehensive functionality of the system may seem trivial." "The customer applications run on hardware with the Linux operating system, and data are all stored in the Oracle database." The company uses hundreds of servers in two data centers in San Jose and Sacramento.

PayPal has grown extremely fast, so to meet the demands of both hardware and human resources is one of the challenging issues since the company went into operation four years ago. Geiger admitted that the site had some problems, so the architecture of the site has been reconstructed to isolate the fault may be more effective. Actually speaking, all based on PayPal's site which Geiger describes as "a security infrastructure mixed with firewalls and encryption method."

Large number of employees and the complexity of PayPal's technology is aimed at curbing cheating. According to Geiger, "could face the most powerful in our system is its ability to fight fraud, and fraudulent handling features instant (real-time). Total number of employees with customer support functions, ensure the reliability is over 800 people that focused on fighting fraud. "

In establishing an online payment system successfully, the problem of how to create a solid security measures more difficult than against the system makes it convenient and easy for users .
Since its merger with eBay, PayPal's payment system

has appeared in more than 70% of auction site Ebay. PayPal is now handling the payment of up to 360 USD per second

Led by co-founder Max Levchin, a core team of 30 engineers (many of them still work in the company) has been programming and original software maintenance PayPal.

Currently, Levchin has left PayPal, but he is best known for inventing algorithms security and fraud prevention to help companies overcome many of the big time before the collapse of style dot.com movement. Is a code writer, who turns 23 years old when Levchin co-founded the company in 1998 along with Peter Thiel, former CEO of financial services.

The company focuses mainly on making the transaction type is using P2P networks to bank and credit card electronic availability, control the phenomenon of cheating. But what is most essential is to find a basic software, a set of algorithms working in real time to quickly detect the phenomenon of cheating in the system.

Igor was named after the Russian criminals who were caught in 2000 with the help of PayPal, this algorithm is the company's proprietary and written in C + +. Their basic function is to check for abnormalities in a variety of checking in a transaction. "Any time you access it," Geiger said, "The checkpoint will see who you are, you want to transfer money to whom and from where. After all the testing, the software will determine by our algorithms to see transactions that have questionable phenomenon or not. " This process is nearly identical to the system check the credit card fraud, which compares previous sales history of customers to identify a payment transaction is too large or a more unusual shopping round.

As important as technology, human interaction is also a protection ring Monday to limit fraud. Whenever the software is suspect fraud, it will convert the transaction for an employee to check by direct contact with customers. This also is what Geiger called a control type "almost immediately", which led PayPal to hire a large number of personnel trained to detect fraud.

Currently, the immediate challenge of technology with PayPal is to maintain a solid success with its rapid P2P services and transactions, to become an online payment solution for merchants larger . The next step on PayPal's technology will not work towards developing new features in the system because in reality, the apparent simplicity of the system is the key to the success of PayPal.

Instead, PayPal's purpose here is how the large trader access to this payment system. This new project will be to develop a set of system application programming interface (API) to PayPal's partners can write programs and design Web pages that interact with PayPal's data via XML. Allowing third parties to integrate their sites with the PayPal system is an important part in the strategy of the company, in order to attract big names to use PayPal as their payment system.

Supporting factors behind the success of PayPal is actually just a simple formula: take heavy bags to the customers (merchants) pay for services, but everyone is free to use the service, so that free customers will do the marketing chain style for those who register to purchase using PayPal.
Most of PayPal's revenue from the transaction account and the provision of goods and services often through PayPal. PayPal revenue from 2.2 to 2.7% of the selling price plus a transaction fee of 30 cents. Although individuals hold the money in your account at PayPal, but the company is not banking without interest because of this money. In fact, financial condition and business prospects of PayPal is great, the company has entered the stock market successfully since February 2002, the worst period for any new company listing any listed business in the Internet field.

However, the dominance of companies in the P2P payments depend very much on the success of the marketing in the network. Previously, PayPal has paid to use 5 to 10 dollars if they get more customers, friends registered to use PayPal. As more consumers realized the convenience and safety of these services, they drew a lot of other people involved in the global system PayPal, and speed has now reached 28,000 new accounts per day .

Unlike most other business sites, companies rely on word of mouth marketing style and not make the campaign hype, rhetoric to build their own brand from scratch 0.

PayPal partly because, in part because PayPal is a pioneer in currency trading model entirely new, the company has always been the banks and the authorities "to do" thoroughly. Some investigators probe whether the funds transferred by whom to whom, and for what goods or services whatsoever. PayPal makes money by just two people together, so this payment system has been used for some suspicious activity. In fact, in 2002, the U.S. Attorney's Office has accused PayPal of violating 9 / 11 Patriot Act (patriotic), and Betting Control Act by intentionally allowing the payment transaction for the evaluation activities money abroad. Payments for online gambling was extinguished when eBay took over officially in October 10-2002 PayPal, but PayPal is time to admit that these transactions that contributed to 6% of their income.

When tracking the bad guys use PayPal to pay for the operation of illegal offline, Geiger admitted that "strictly prevent this kind of behavior is very difficult. We've got the algorithm to find them . For example if you transfer money in many different accounts, which will cause suspicion and agencies are required by law we must follow immediately, whatever are found to report on database federation. "

And also by regular PayPal user's account and credit

card information, it will be attractive to scammers. A common scam is to send an email with this year's logo and address feedback similar to PayPal, in which the notification that their account has been locked and they must enter all the information about a bank account and your credit card.

Besides the announcement and pledged to users that the company never requests customer information in one place other than the company's website, PayPal is also against the hoax by the press for users know when someone suspicious access to their accounts. PayPal address is often a hacker attack, including criminal gangs from Nigeria, Russia and Indonesia, who sought to create a virtual account and used the stolen credit cards in the system.

Despite an absolute success, PayPal is still a controversial companies in the Web world. PayPal We are under attack and blame from both sides: the scammers are trying to exploit the technology of illegally PayPal and the user some questions about the security measures to combat fraud PayPal.
Several opposition websites and
http://www.paypalwarning.com/
http://www.paypalsucks.com/ have collected very quickly scary stories, complaints and lawsuits against PayPal .
Indeed, ingenuity and risk of PayPal is that it balances two often conflicting needs of each online exchange market: an open, easily accessible to anyone who can create an account , billing and receiving payments in

minutes, but should also have anti-fraud measures closely to ensure that the account was created it was real easy, and the transaction is legal.

PayPal continues to grow despite pressure from criminals and consumers. Along with the main Google and eBay, PayPal is one of the few dot-com companies are increasingly powerful. In the first quarter of 2003, before being sold to eBay, PayPal has a substantial profit, revenue increased 248% over the same period in 2002. Currently, over 70% of eBay's auctions are items that allows payment through PayPal.

While the dot-com success famous as Amazon.com and eBay itself became more stable, PayPal is one last miracle story about the Web that success never stop signs again.

The secret of success for Adidas

in the early 70's, the new Adidas started to take over the world's hegemonic position, and so far it has not be ceded to any one maker of sports shoes else in the world.

Adolfe Datxle established sports shoe company Adidas in 1949, after the 2nd world war ended four years. At that time in Europe also are focused on recovery, healing the wounds of war and sports competitions should not have to attract large masses.

Have more than 20 years later, in the early 70's, the new Adidas started to take over the world's hegemonic position, and so far it has not be ceded to any one maker of sports shoes else in the world.

Even wearing a pair of Adidas sports shoes became a way of dressing the world's millions of young people, of all ages, creating a neatly dressed, healthy, in line with strong growth era.

Adidas shoes despite high prices, but also to penetrate and dominate the market in Vietnam, won the popular world of youth sports and Vietnam.
International business has been concluded two secret power of creating market penetration of the Adidas International:

1. Of production to create products unique in shape and color.

Adidas built a great emphasis on laboratory techniques and new materials in order to constantly improve, enhance product quality, attractive styling. The company has many innovative improvements such as sharks do get leather in the shoes of kangaroo skin soft and get to the outer shell, etc. .. In these shoes to run at high speed, Adidas has created grooves in the sole and nylon soles ... It always improves the small details to create favorable conditions for athletes to use.

2. Of consumption, the company has cleverly combined between consumption and advertising propaganda.

Adolfe great attention to international sporting events. At the international sports competitions in Montréal (Canada), we published a very interesting news: 82.8% of medal-winning athletes have used clothing and sporting goods firm Adidas . Shortly after this success, its sales reached one billion dollars.

Adolfe won 80% of total advertising costs for various types of live ads, ads by the athletes perform, only 20% by means of advertising on television, radio.

To take a position gained on the international market, Adidas has conducted a variety of products, not only produce sport shoes, but also produce enough clothes, all, football, football and tennis rackets , the style, these bags for the athletes during competition ...
We must not forget the football teams plus Germany are equipped with all Adidas products won the championship cup football world. Since then, Adidas became the

symbol of the championship.

To be able to expand into a corporate scale as today, Adidas had to apply many industries in the marketplace, from the timing to release the product to change strategies to adapt to the time.

Advertising is an industry that is always young. But at Adidas, youth has become a corporate culture, to make nuclear penetration of the company. The average age of employees is 32 Adidas, and the staff that came from over 40 countries. Town of Herzogenaurach, Adidas headquarters which was abbreviated as "Herzo." And the common language used here is English.

Step into the headquarters' Herzo ", will see a row of offices behind the cafeteria noise. Adidas workers in this place is called "house football." Here, every barrel linoleum were piled into 3 blocks. Corridor stacking cardboard boxes. Memo next to the stairs plastered with pieces of newspapers from around the world, referring to the contribution of the Adidas World Cup 2006 in Germany.

This building is home owner Gunter Weigl. "3 stripes and bar has seeped into my DNA," the man said he came from Bavaria. Like many other pillars of character elite ranks of Adidas, Weigl was sticking with the company over 15 years.

All questions related to football, all it takes to answer Weigl, such as Adidas will sponsor any teams? What stars? Funding contracts should be renewed and the contract should end? Austria's players will have the design like? Will be produced where? ...

Weigl gathered about 100 people were eager to project the World Cup. Those who are selected for this activity has signed a confidentiality agreement in absolute secrecy. Common sense, the products are kept for as long, as one would expect when it is sold.

But in the context of globalization today, the secret is not always successful. This is the reality that the cognitive strategies when Adidas announced the decision to put the name of their World Cup ball.

Adidas has convinced the veteran character introduced in FIFA ball at the draw for World Cup finals in Leipzig on 9/12/2005. This means that 4 million balls will be produced and transported to the secret corners of the world on that day. Also with how to organize the same as publishing the new Harry Potter, the U.S. subsidiary will be released simultaneously on this product. Planning timeframes allow disparities to 9 hours.

To avoid their eyes of customs officials' preferred

annoying, "Adidas had to transport a large number of fake ball from Thailand. Globally, the retailer was ordered not to open the seal affixed to the barrel to a certain point, though there are found several days earlier.

Just to set the monitoring time, the senior representative of Adidas in each region a special card with the new ball was introduced right: that is contrary to the players, Michael Ballack will be awarded to the host Heidi Klum on stage. And with two security fences guarding, the ball has really become a precious crown.

There are also some omissions occur in this process, but did not cause major consequences. For example, in Istanbul, a clerk inadvertently displayed this ball up the price of the Adidas three days before the time allowed. Even in Herzo, not all goes smoothly: the morning of 9 / 2, a ball called "Teamwork" was exhibited at the main entrance of the headquarters.

Times change - change tactics.

"It sounds like something from another planet," says Karl Heinz Lang, an experienced shoe maker said. Lang to Herzogenaurach in the 1970s. Then, he was responsible for establishing and supervising the production of shoes in the Adidas factories in foreign countries, especially in the USSR. Adidas this period is not yet known, it was only a family company, with activities focusing on "product, not marketing."

In the 1974 World Cup, players representing over 85% 3 bar striped shoes. What they wear above the ankle is secondary. For example, nobody thought anything when players, Johan Cruyff Holland tore a bar in 3 striped Adidas shirt off before the final against Germany. It is an expression of protest, perhaps simply because the captain of the Netherlands has a contract with Puma.

The German player then has competed in the lily white shirt, and no striped bar. That's what the German Football Federation wants. Union officials, led by president Hermann Neuberger was defending victims against commercialization in sports.

"We're not even allowed to print logos on clothing," Lang recalls. As one of the last person to work with the founder of Adidas - Adolf Dassler, the village has a first floor office at the shoe factory Scheinfeld, the headquarters of Adidas about 48 km to the west.

In the past, this place had more than 1,200 employees. But now, it became a museum of the Karl Heinz Lang Adidas with a guide. In the display cabinets of hundreds of shoes that Adidas sports stars has brought in history. Lang pierced white gloves on before getting out of the box of memorabilia.

Each pair of shoes were to tell viewers a story and are

recounted Lang: a dark brown pair of sprint athlete Jesse Owens American, who won four gold medals at the 1936 Olympics in Berlin; boots the other is the old West German captain Fritz Walter brought in World Cup finals in 1954, also has double yellow Lothar Matthaus' bring in the 1990 World Cup finals.

Then he locked coffin "treasures" this back and walked across the room, but Adidas is intended to accommodate customers located close to the special pair of shoes according to personal preference. One special pair of Adidas that are packaged for David Beckham, the name of a player signing for the Adidas ad. Those shoes are embroidered the name of Beckham's third son by red: Brooklyn, Romeo and Cruz.

Zippo - cool flames of gender.

Zippo is one of America's specialty. Nickel-plated lighter joskin looks even relatively inconvenient as big and heavy, cumbersome as for the pocket, jacket pocket. Yet it has existed for more than a prestigious three-quarters of a century, confirmed the location history is not only in America but also in almost everywhere in the world.

It is famous that Zippo just say that everyone understand it as a lighter. Seen from a different aspect, it is also flame illuminates a hidden corner in the heart of America is rife with complex events that Americans want to bury into oblivion, including the Vietnam War.

The advent of Zippo

Zippo is the father of George G. Blaisdell. Born on 06.05.1895 in Bradford, Pennsylvania, George G. Blaisdell, floating on the surface, are considered more successful in reaping the most difficult years of the Great Depression happened in America since 24/10/1929. He was at school and hated school.

He left school in grade 5 and declared flatly that family will never go to school anymore. Then, his father sent him to a military academy in hopes his son will be better educated with military discipline of steel. However, George G. Blaisdell also just finished the second year of the Academy and left school just before school dismissal decision school.

Frustrated with the education of son, father of George G. Blaisdell took him to work in family business: The Company mechanical Blaisdell. Here, George G. Blaisdell study of metals, metal processing with virtuoso skill that almost 30 years later become valuable platform for the launch of the Zippo lighter.

George G. Blaisdell, Zippo's father.

After the First World War one, George G. Blaisdell began managing the family business. He sold the business and invest the entire proceeds to the oil industry.

But even then oil industry as well as all the other economies falling into recession spiral of the Great Depression. And in this context, George G. Blaisdell founded Zippo decision in 1932 on the righteous homeland. His decision had been regarded as foolish and impossible.

Sarah Dorn - daughter of George G. Blaisdell has been said about his father and the early days of Zippo like this: "My father hated the work related to oil. He was not good at this field. He also did not have the qualities for the same things. The only thing he knew in the 30 years of the 20th century that he must do something, because this is an extremely difficult time, stress. At that time he did not have much money.

He should favor people who have money to open its production company Zippo lighters. No one believes in his ideas. And at that time, his plan is really stupid. Please imagine if a person produces and sells a lighter silly money prices which could feed a family for a long time during the Great Depression, they may say they do not also lose crazy location. So what made him determined to do?. In my opinion, it is tinged with despair and recklessness. He must do this for themselves and their families, because, at that time no other way. "

The first Zippo George G. Blaisdell began late in 1932 and completed in early 1933. On the lighter has the hand-engraved for George G. Blaisdell wrote: "The first Zippo, forbidden to touch the exhibits." Currently it is on display at the Museum of Zippo in Bradford.

Since then, tens of million Zippo has been processed and is present in almost all over the world. It would also open a museum to showcase and celebrate it.
Zippo Museum

Founded in 1997, to date, Zippo Museum in Bradford - Penncylvania has attracted millions of visitors. The heart of the museum are 75 unique Zippo made special anniversary of the establishment of Zippo. Man who has spent millions to be the owner of the collection is unique, but not satisfied, because, as George G. Blaisdell said: "There are things that come out is not for sale."

Zippo museum in America.

Come to the museum, visitors also enjoy a fun thing to do anymore is himself a Zippo for himself or friends and relatives. With these embryos box, gears, gorgeous, and the hollow body to provide detailed of skilled workers, only a short time you will become owner of a Zippo is one of a kind. Because, whether you have to manually make the second car, it can not completely identical to the first.

It is also the principle of "uniqueness" in the business motto of Zippo.

If you have the opportunity to travel to Bradford, do not miss the opportunity. Please provide your address below: 1932 Zippo Drive Bradford, PA 16701.

Ignition Zippo - "very professional and sophisticated game"

Zippo how ignition is considered to be manifested in the population level playing Zippo worldwide. If only the ignition in the usual way is open, his finger on a thorn gears to emit sparks, the "level" is "as low as cockroaches" (the language of stylish people playing). According to statistics there are nearly a hundred types of ignition Zippo. Who can skillfully ignited by all 10 fingers. Withdrawal lighters out of the bag is already on fire. At any position which may spark.

But not mean much compared to other super players. " With "sophisticated upper surplus", they can fire in all parts of the body, even with all ... tongue. If anyone ever go to Japan would know about the Kabukichyo - one of the world-famous playboy of Tokyo. There is a far-famed character named Masatoshi Kamimura. As a male flight attendant in a cellar in Kabukichyo, Kamimura is known to most people sell more goods, the highest income among the attendants at the level of "noble" in Japan. His income is at more than $ 30,000 a night. This is because wage income plus commissions earned from the amount of wine, beer, cigarettes sold that night.

Kamimura has graceful movements cocktails, style attractive, intelligent, understanding. But "unique way" is his Zippo art ignition. A lady just to shop, draw out a cigarette hand, Kamimura immediately appeared from nowhere and nobody knows where he to lighter, with a mystical movement, as attractive as magician David Corperphin, flames erupted from the sleeve after the words "ti i. ... i.. inh" lasted very clear characteristics of Zippo. The pleasant surprise to rise further when Kamimura pulled his hand out of his pocket that had a flickering flame on two fingers as if he hid technology available to fire people when necessary, so naturally drawn.

Of the Kamimura Zippo performances only really starts at midnight, at which visitors became more excited after several weeks of alcohol. Handsome face full of masculine, foot flexibility and confidence of those who know they have dominated, with soft Kamimura or Valse seductive tango performance by sparking a series of unique Zippo applause fence fence applause.

It is also named for the way his firing by naming abilities in the martial arts. For example, the ignition of two Zippo hands, his words in the book out in front and then offered to customers is called "the god who donated fruit" (ie gods offered gibbon fruit.). Also the lighter from a secret place and then suddenly fire upon her is called "Single of the Dragon" (Dragon hang out) ... etc etc ... To be sitting and chatting and watching Kamimura Zippo Games, the ladies, he must pay to 700USD/H

With nearly 8 years of pain, turned the ignition Kamimura Zippo into performing arts can be picked out of money.

Zippo - corner flame from the past

And who knows, Zippo lighter is a very simple, square, shiny shell plating Crome, used gear, flint and fuel, but so acute that just snap your fingers is a flame to flare up together with English "blowing" the clear when the lid popped out or closed. Can be used in all weather conditions with incredible durability. Therefore, it is appropriate to take a trip.

During the Vietnam War, an estimated hundreds of thousands of the Zippo by foot soldiers in Vietnam. But in Vietnam, more than a Zippo lighter. Zippo flame flickering light field tent at night to dispel the fear, empty. It is also a friend confided in the heart of the lonely. Expeditionary soldiers, with the mood of the people be deceived, exploited to the goals unjust, immoral Zippo has carved on its own line of thought, even his downfall. Accordingly, the Zippo became witnesses speak about the mood of American soldiers in the Vietnam War. They are hidden in the symbol of what many Americans have realized from a stark view of the task is marked in red a force

These words contain both bitter contempt yourself:

"Whether I go mid valley covered shadow of death, I'm not scared because I was demon demon most heinous of this valley."
"Death is my job and now work right."
Or self-consoled himself:
"I'm not scared, just lonely."
"Please do not tell me about Vietnam because I've been there"
"We, the soul is not self-giving prayer, lack of education by those who lead, are doing the unnecessary for the ungrateful man."
Like the sun or moon said:
"We do not live or die, we just smoke and fly into."
"You'll never really lived until he nearly died."
"If mi get it (the Zippo) from the see of us, we hope it will bring luck to mi like it is giving us. "
And to finally let slip a vulgar way, but full of "American nature" of a naked truth but has been exploring lately:
"Killing for peace is fucking for virginity" (roughly translated: to kill peacekeepers like sex to preserve virginity.)

Perhaps with the inscriptions on, no further comment is enough to understand the nature of the mind of the American soldier Vietnam War. Perhaps until now, many Americans still shocked, bewildered every time you hear "ti .. i inh ... .." no where to be and at closing the lid of the Zippo. As the prayer bell It reminded me a dark stretch

Born during the Great Depression America's dark, Zippo is considered to be an array of light, a ray of hope and an optimistic definition of man. Currently, full-scale crisis is spreading worldwide with no less severity of what the Great Depression in 1929's America. Hopefully this is the time for something similar will Zippo was born, creating a new array of bright, even as small as a halo of fire in the bitter winter night Zippo. Accordingly, assets of humanity will become richer than the middle of the great loss today.

Sony's secret of success.

1 / 1958, Akio Morita decided to rename the company into technical communication Totsuko Sony - an unusual event in the business world by the Japanese before, not one company in the country is named after the word Latin. Just a few years later, Morita became well known, is the idol of the young.

His business career began when Sony all round he was 25. At that time, Morita graduated from Osaka University physicist. But he did not follow the traditional family that he has 14 previous generation pursued, that alcohol production lines Sake. In 1946, Akio Morita and Masaru friend Ibuka engineers founded the company in communications technology Totsuko with only 20 employees and capital of 190,000 yen.

Morita said: "The first motivation and most importantly helped me establish a firm desire to bring friends and his employees a stable work environment where they can devote bulb blood, brains and heart to devote to the development of society, the economy recover after the war. "

After World War II, Japan was devastated, few people believe that Japanese goods could compete with American goods. The first project the company is buying a camcorder Totsuko German disc weighs about 50 kg is pulled out, research to improve the camera's compact discs and more selling. But the work of the whole company at that time may evolve. Then Morita decided to establish a wide network of trade and thereby capture the areas not yet have opponents. In 1950, his company launched the first type of recorder in Japan branded G-Type, 5 years after the first transistor radios, called TR-55.

After the name was changed to Sony in 1958, the company has begun to penetrate the U.S. market, not through intermediaries. Sony has increasingly be profitable not only due to market consumer products of high quality but also because of the technical invention. In 1960, Sony launched the first TV semiconductor in the world, three years later was the first semiconductor VCR.

Dated 6/6/1961, Sony became the first Japanese companies have shares listed on the New York stock market price per share is $ 17.5. Even in the first session, 2 million shares were sold, the closing price that day shot up to 24 dollars. In 1979, a pocket music player Walkman brand was born to conquer the world. In late 1989, Sony bought Columbia Pictures (a major U.S. film studios were founded in 1924) for $ 4.8 billion. This event shook the business world and the world.

When asked about the secret of the success of Sony, Mr. Morita has shown the following key points:

1. Robot applications in production lines.

"Many people believe that Japan is the leading exporter in the world and is also the capital of the world's largest lenders because they work more than Westerners. The reality is not like that, we work Most are around 1800-1900 hours per year. We stay three weeks in a year.

Genuine Sony first made this idle and virtually all enterprises, Japanese companies have applied so. Today most Japanese people have 2 to 3 weeks off work, they spend that time to travel, play sports, learn a culture, art ...

Japanese problem why our success is that we work longer hours, not other peoples work that is not efficient because we have robots in every stage of the production line. For example, in one of our factory is located in

Bayonne (France), production work has always run continuously seven days a week, 24 hours a day, but visitors will find this tour very quiet because the machine 've done everything. Profits and production is thus increased. "

2. There are always new products, weird, beautiful.

"Before the rise of the increasingly powerful dragons of Asia, Japan has nothing to worry about. We've got a long way to go before the world of electronic engineering, computer science. We also is the world's leading countries in research and industrial development. Many people make the mistake to think that Japan would lose the prices of Japan's rising market. new products, good will always triggers curiosity of consumers, although there was pressure to sell at high prices also will be quickly consumed in greater numbers.

In addition to items such as orchestra computer hifi, video, we also develop products in television, video, information technology, semiconductors, radio cassette, electronics for the public and for professionals ".

3. Pay attention to our customers.

"The Japanese manufacturers have been paying attention to customers, always creating the trust clients and therefore consumers, even in anywhere in the world prefer to use more Japanese goods."

4. Want to know the best product possible for foreign goods.

"As the owner of a firm's reputation in Japan, but my Japanese is not only found in Japan. Our motto is to produce better goods must be of good use. Just good, then buying used goods, without distinction of any water produced. I myself have a helicopter in France, a Mercedes car from Germany. tennis balls, tennis bags bearing the La Coste my, my luggage bag is Wilton's products. "

The secret of success of McDonald's

Once outside the 50, only two dozen in the last years, Raymond Kroc made a miracle full of legends. He alone has created the popular fast food corporations and the world's largest.

Unannounced great idea

Raymond Kroc full name is Raymond Albert Kroc, he was born October 5, 1902 at Oak, Illinois, USA. Finishing Year 10, Ray Kroc made driving an ambulance with little innate musical, he played piano in restaurants and clubs. 20 years old, he was accepted as the true run for its sales Lily Tulip Cup.

More than a dozen years later, Ray Kroc met Earl Prince, the boss of a company distributing blender. He has pulled Ray Kroc on do it yourself. And Ray Kroc was the selling machine nearly two dozen vitamins for years. Ray Kroc made just enough for a normal life and looks like he will accept what you have. By Ray Kroc had turned 52, and he began his intention to retire.

Until one day late in 1954, Ray Kroc to small fast food restaurant in San Bernadino in California, American West. He was very glad, when brothers Richard and Maurice McDonald bought at the instant a dozen Prince blender.

What Ray Kroc was particularly impressed by the small shops, but customers lining up more than 20 meters. Try eating Hamburger, Ray Kroc was very tasty, simple, reasonable price. Closer, saw two brothers Raymond McDonald and processing organizations are serving the industrial looks. 8 found blender, each row containing 5 units can shake a glass of milk for 40 times.

Fries as well as a dozen pieces. Cups, plates are used for paper should not bother most people clean and wash stages. Upon returning home, an idea, but the great surprise was flashed in his head of sales has experienced over 50. Why I can not cooperate with the brothers to open more stores McDolnald similar.

Immediately, Ray Kroc sold off the blender. No need to

take more time and paper and pen, he has completed a development plan for a fast food chain stores on the basis of the McDonald brothers in San Bernadino. Ray Kroc natural comparison shop your system will act as the industrial production lines much less automobile production lines of Henry Ford. And he will become a revolutionary way for fast food industry like Henry Ford opened the way for the auto industry in America and the world.

Do think, Ray Kroc started to implement new ideas to seem utopian ambitions. Speak with financial dexterity of a salesman, marketing veteran, Ray Kroc convinced the brothers Richard and Maurice McDonald for his cooperation. Accordingly, Ray Kroc was all right to use the name McDonald's fast food system will develop in the franchise business franchising. Richard and Maurice will receive 1% of sales of this store. McDonald's System Inc. company. operated by Ray Kroc founded.

It looks like Ray Kroc discovered he was too little time, so he rushed to work. The idea of perfection as the franchising business model and flowing at the same time. Ray Kroc fast development model with a business philosophy of its own. According to him, happiness is the result of sweat, as sweat poured many people will be happier.

Ray Kroc is well prepared, methodical and confident that it will succeed. Dated 2/3/1955, fast-food restaurant's first McDolnald opened by Ray Kroc opened in De Plaines,

Illinois. He was active family, relatives and close friends, each person owns a shop to simultaneously launched the restaurant McDolnald's sizes are different but identical to the organization, product, form color signs.

Amazing miracle of the birth of the fast food industry initiated by McDolnald's start from there really. Within five years there were 200 McDonald's restaurants were opened in several places and are well received.

success story of McDonald's.

In 1961, Ray Kroc was a bold decision to buy back 1% of revenue rights as agreed previously. After much negotiation, McDonald brothers have agreed to receive 2.7 million to Ray Kroc alone the name McDonald's and enjoy the exclusive right of return of the McDonald's system.

To get this money, Ray Kroc had to borrow a lot, including many in the venture capital fund. If Ray Kroc's decision is considered one of the business decisions the greatest, or be put into the business curriculum, to the brothers Richard and Maurice McDonald is wrong. If not, they can now receive up to $ 200 million on revenue of

Franchising model of McDonald's corporation is a big advantage for franchisees and business autonomy huge. The store owner can choose their own activities advertising, marketing appropriate for the area, your location. One secret of success of particular importance is the McDonald's Corporation has put the issue on the rental store business model of franchising. Shop area outside the larger the license fee franchise, corporation also collects large sums respectively.

Thanks to that style that Ray Kroc had to overcome a difficult financial situation to control sales of franchisees. To do this, McDonald's is actively searching the grounds beautiful location, convenient for business. On the other hand, McDonald's is a strategic long-term business cooperation with large corporate partners such as Coca Cola and consumption become the world's largest Coca-Cola.

Ray Kroc was interested in the industrialization of the production stage. McDonald's boss to pay special attention to these factors: quality and sanitation services and confirmed that the key advantage thanks to industrialization. Ray Kroc also invested in a laboratory in Chicago specializing in evaluation of quality, hygiene, food safety.

Since 1967, McDonald's began expanding overseas. To succeed, Ray Kroc had to be very flexible tactics, without losing the image of fast food industry, called McDonald's. Muslim countries with McDonald's, then add lamb dish with fried bread, the name is Arabic is "McMaharadscha", or "McFalafel." With the Indians do not eat beef, there are dishes to be replaced with modified Hamburger fried chicken.

Decode the success of L'Oréal cosmetics

Born in 1907, L'Oréal (France) is leading the world cosmetics market of sales and satisfaction you may have. Differentiation of products has always been maintained for over 100 years.

L'Oréal was born from the idea of a talented engineer living in the capital of Paris (France) - Eugene Schueller. He invented the artificial hair dyes first in 1907. A year later he began his business with the advent of the French hair dye company and he was born into L'Oréal. When the company was only one person only is Mr. Eugene Schueller.

Eugene all night to manufacture dyes, while the day is going to sell to stores throughout the city. Period of consolidation has been carried out. With a small investment from an accountant, in 1909, Eugene buy a larger apartment and hired his first employee. He began his advertising magazines hair care, La Coiffure de Paris. Then in 1934, L'Oréal has enough financial resources to acquire a French company named Monsaron other.

This step is the launch pad to launch Eugene a more creative breakthroughs of the L'Oréal - shampoo contains no soap. However, instead of continuing to use the brand L'Oréal shampoo, he has given it a separate brand name - DOP. Since then, the company's Eugene constantly receiving and creates different kinds of products. In 1960, the company bought & Garnier, Lancome, then launched Guy Laroche fragrances. Today, this brand stands behind the leading brand of the perfume world, such as Ralph Lauren, Giorgio Armani and Lancôme. L'Oréal is also the leading brand in the cosmetics market, owns the Maybelline brand products along with product line of L'Oréal.

The secret of success of L'Oréal is a difference in the characteristics of each brand. Maybelline is such contact with the young and powerful way of New York, despite the fact that the product of a French company. L'Oréal has made his reputation as the "United Nations of beauty" are counted separately by various co-exist in a global company. As illustrated article on Business Week magazine - "L'Oréal: The Beauty of Global Branding", edition dated 06/28/1999 - the secret of L'Oréal is the transfer capability "a fascination with different cultures" through the many products of this brand.

Article wrote: "... Whether they sell the flower of Italian pride, chic look of New York or the elegance of the French through their brands, L'Oréal has always been to reach more people with sufficient income and from many different cultures, than any other cosmetic companies in the world. This has made L'Oréal distinct companies with a monotonous, such as Coca-Cola - a company with a single brand for sale worldwide. "

Chairman of the Board of the British - Lindsay Owen-Jones, L'Oréal, said: "We were conscious efforts to diversify the cultural origins of their brands." For example, when the company acquired Maybelline Company for $ 758 million in 1996, L'Oréal has carefully preserved American pronunciation of the brand, and launching sub-brands, like Maybelline Miami Chill and television advertising in Manhattan. This strategy has proved its effectiveness. By early 2003, the Maybelline sales force doubled, the brand was stronger than the time before the transfer, and their reputation well beyond U.S. borders.

L'Oréal has demonstrated that the determination of national identity for the brand does not limit the success of our international. In fact, by adding personality to the brand, this strategy is two-dimensional effects at the same time.

One point worth mentioning is that, L'Oréal is not afraid to eat something from each other between their products. When a company has multiple products or brands of the same type or the same market, there is concern that this brand will probably swallow each other alive. L'Oréal has developed and become so big that became his main rival. But Owen-Jones said that he wanted to create the atmosphere of tension between the marketing group, which is the pressure needed for self-developed brands. "An atmosphere of urgency and challenge is what we are looking for," he says today with toBusiness Week.

So, Owen-Jones has established a headquarters in New York the other, a "resource center for" separate and distinct from "base" of the company in Paris. Such measures were to prevent any complacency that, even in those areas that dominate the L'Oréal. The company has experienced growth during its first decades, more than any other competitor, but Owen-Jones has said that he was never satisfied and convinced that the company's I'm succeeding. The main internal competition like this is a pressure form a continuous creative environment.

To ensure that your brand becomes different, L'Orreal not only emphasized the national character of the brand but also collapse them. Today, they only focus on five main product areas: hair care, hair dye, cosmetics, fragrances and skin care. Under the administration of the Owen-Jones, the number of global brands of L'Oréal has been narrowed further. The brand is the product classification from the public, such as Maybelline, until the special luxury products, such as Helena Rubinstein. But they still maintain a strong personality of his own by force of L'Oréal no need to create a brand name means everything for everyone.

L'Oréal is probably the best brand is expanding the range of products with the same origin of these international companies. Its brand targeted at both men and women with many different types of products. Personality of the brand, from an original idea by Eugene Schueller, a French flair in harmony with scientific expertise. L'Oréal brand not only the position of such a product that everyone can use, but also as a personal reward that consumers deserve.

"Because you deserve" is the slogan of L'Oréal ad, is spoken by stars like Ben Affleck and Jennifer Aniston in the TV ads have recently summarized the characteristics of this brand. Like all of the company itself, her brand into the global personal computer, said at the same time directly to the individual and the entire market, because both can not be separated from each other.

However, the "exclusivity" is perhaps the strategic themes of L'Oréal. Each company's brand retains its own character with their own brand names. In this way, L'Oréal can achieve the best results of both the business world, can always keep the brand strong while work continues to expand, against the temptations of the package ghem all brands and products into a homogenous under the banner of L'Oréal. L'Oréal what proved to be: in the world today with the market is constantly being split and the creation of different brands, instead of a single brand for all, the main the door to come with success.

The secret of success of L'Oréal:

- The breakthrough. The major brand is formed from the break, not from advertising - it only to later.

- Calculate the difference. L'Oréal uses many different brands to attract different markets. Unlike other global brands, L'Oréal has no ambition to create a kingdom with only a single image.

- Bollywood. Because there are many brands for many different markets, L'Oréal does not hesitate exaggerated personalities of their brands, while other brands fear that the expansion will affect the brand main.
- Consolidation. L'Oréal does not roll out a new brand just because you want to do that, but they only invest in the brands already available or received through the markets have been thoroughly studied.

- Nationality . Many brands try to hide their nationality because of concern that this would lose the advantage of some products in foreign markets. L'Oréal is the opposite, they are ready to show off the character country or region after its brand name, such as L'Oréal Maybelline New York or Paris.

Pepsi - brand differentiation

Pepsi show with everything from carbonated beverages, from the taste, the choice to feel pleasure, fun and youthful. All those things were from the Pepsi ads and led to the development of the Pepsi slogan "Exciting with Pepsi" in America and "Ask for More" - "desire more than" in other countries.

MARKET.

Today, Pepsi is becoming ever more popular. According to the survey, the four products carbonated drinks are sold in the world is a product of Pepsi, Pepsi a day in total sold over 200 million products and this number continues to increase.

Properties worldwide, customers pay about 32 billion dollars for items of soft drink Pepsi-Cola. Every year, an American consumer drinks about 55 gallons of carbonated water, what makes the U.S. as the country consumed beverage world's largest.

In Europe, the figure is more modest, at nearly 12 gallons of gas, but water consumption is increasing steadily - carbonated water is gradually becoming an important part in water solution thirsty here.

Achievements.

Pepsi-Cola Company with headquarters in Purchase, New York, as part of corporate global beverage PepsiCo, Inc.. Last year, PepsiCo earned more than U.S. $ 200 billion and become the leading provider of sales and net profits for retailers in America.

Caleb Bradham, a pharmacy in New Bern, North Carolina invented Pepsi in the early years of the 20th century. The soda dispensing a sort of success he has achieved immediately and shortly thereafter, Pepsi-Cola Company was founded.

Originated from the very ordinary, Pepsi has survived bankruptcy twice and became the company's No. 2 beverage in the world. Today, the symbol of the Pepsi globe logo is one of the most known worldwide. The beverages of Pepsi-Cola can be found everywhere in over 195 countries worldwide.

HISTORICAL DEVELOPMENT.

In 1886, Bradham can not understand the level of success of Pepsi in the future when he prepared an easy target drink made from the carbonate, sugar, vanilla and a little oil. It is sold in the region under the name "Brad's Drink" Bradham in 1893 but changed to a new name "Pepsi-Cola", listen to exciting, energetic, stronger and prepared to offer a broad sell more.

Pepsi prosperity over the next two decades. But due to the transport, due to lack of production lines and some other difficulties in World War I caused the company's bankruptcy. The new owner has restored to the company but in 1931, the economic situation drastically weakened once again make the company bankrupt.

At that moment, Charles Guth, president of Loft Industries - a system of candy stores and soda water, has acquired the business of Pepsi and bring it to sell in the shops of his. To save, he has used 12-ounce bottle of beer containers and a bottle of Pepsi sold for 10 cents, while carbonated drinks are sold in standard 6-ounce size bottles. To increase sales, reduce costs Guth has yet to leave 5cent/chai 12-ounce bottles, keep the Pepsi differences with competitors.

In 1938, Walter Mack was selected to become the new president of Pepsi-Cola and not long after, he launched a new ad for 12-ounce bottle of Pepsi with more rhyming song "Nickel, Nickel". This song quickly became popular and was recorded with 55 different languages. The song changed to "Pepsi-Cola Hits The Spot" and his song - LIFE magazine in 1940 were rated "bad songs nodding."

After World War 2 and the next 50 years, Alfred Steele responsible for the expansion of each stage in the development business. With the economic changes in the gas sector beverages, Pepsi has adopted the standard pricing and brand strategy to become full cau.Do is when Pepsi bottles made strange and twisted round campaign New Report "Be sociable, Have a Pepsi" (more comfortable with Pepsi). Initiatives that open the way for a campaign focused on young people's Pepsi.

Following that is a different ad breakthrough. Baby-boom generation (those born from 1946 to 1964), which were oriented to the future with optimism high. Pepsi grasp this thought and give the name "Pepsi Generation."

Over the next 30 years, "Pepsi Generation" is still the lodestar in all of the popular Pepsi ads. In 1964, Pepsi also for further products Diet Pepsi with its own great songs and memorable "Girlwatchers" - this song is in the Top 40 best songs. In addition, Mountain Dew - a carbonated soft drink sold only in some areas also made the same year and quickly became a carbonated beverage popular throughout the world.

From 60 to 70 years, Pepsi has started a gigantic success, reducing the gap with other major competitors. All renewal under Mr Don Kendall leaders including releasing the first 2-liter bottle - is made of lightweight plastic, durable and lighter than glass bottles. Company merged with Frito-Lay and moved headquarters to Purchase, NY, a small town outside New York City.

In the mid 70's, Pepsi Challenge was born. The tests showed that many people like the taste of Pepsi over Coke all other countries and not long after that, this program is advertised on TV with Pepsi own style. By

1976, Pepsi-Cola became the single brand of carbonated soft drink sales is highest in American supermarkets and to the early years of the '80s, Pepsi brand soft drinks are the leading many buyers are taking home the most.

During the 80's and 90's, Pepsi ad images by a long list of superstars including Michael Jackson, Tina Turner, Michael J. Fox, Ray Charles and Cindy Crawford.

In 1998, Pepsi 100 year anniversary and launched a new logo for the new millennium - a sphere with 3 blue, white, red, cool blue background, the consistency of the Pepsi logo design worldwide.

PRODUCT.

Position "beverage companies comprehensive" Pepsi is one of the biggest reason for success worldwide. In the U.S., Pepsi-Cola Company has many brands such as Pepsi, Diet Pepsi, Pepsi ONE, Mountain Dew, Wild Cherry Pepsi, Aquafina ... The company also manufactures and sells teas and instant coffee through joint ventures with Lipton and Starbucks. Pepsi's main products are sold worldwide are included Pepsi Max, Mirinda and 7-Up.

The Pepsi-Cola products are of high quality and excellent value. How can people believe that all the bottles and cans of Pepsi always tastes great and fresh? This process begins offering the most accurate components. Then the ingredients are prepared with modern technological processes. Next, the standardization of production processes, product quality and distribution systems of each locality is a complete arrangement to ensure the opening of a bottle / cans of Pepsi at home also makes people feel cool drink cool, refreshing, exciting right now is like buying drinks. It may seem hard to believe but it's true.

RECENT DEVELOPMENTS.

In 2000, Pepsi made the program "Pepsi Challenge", this is a promotional offer attractive nature and capable of convincing all. Consumers are testing samples of carbonated soft drinks and Pepsi's largest competitor, but not labeled, and whether they prefer to answer any more samples. This program is held in hundreds of cities and towns across America, from the center of trade, fairs, outdoor parks to the beach, ballpark and other crowded areas .

Many consumers remember the Pepsi Challenge program was first organized and became the national events in the mid 70's and early 80's. And what exactly on time which, until now still true: the number of people still like the taste of Pepsi majority. For those who do not participate in the program, they are invited to visit www.pepsi.com with detailed instructions to perform the test.

Promotion.

The application of new technology in advertising and promotional signs to distinguish the company's Pepsi-Cola. In fact, the company is seen as leading companies in the field of advertising, marketing, sales and marketing promotions. With the campaign "Joy of Pepsi" Pepsi Exciting to "express the humor, humanity and Pepsi's music with great feeling that can only be brought to the new Pepsi.

The campaign was launched in 1999 with the name "Joy of Cola" and after being renamed the "Joy of Pepsi" campaign has achieved tremendous success in USA TODAY, up to No. 3 of 50 advertising was assessed by USA Today.

Currently, the program has Pepsi ads pop queen Britney Spears to sing a song with the melody of "Joy of Pepsi" and former senator Bob Dole to Congress expressing his love for "the Your little "Pepsi-Cola.

Brand Values

Pepsi show with everything from carbonated beverages, from the taste, the choice to feel pleasure, fun and youthful. All those things were from the Pepsi ads and led to the development of the Pepsi slogan "Exciting with Pepsi" in America and "Ask for More" - "desire more than" in other countries.

Pepsi tries to become more youthful, more unusual and better suited than competitors. That's why Pepsi helps maintain the "simple", "exciting" and "fresh" until now.

What you did not know about Pepsi-Cola
• In 1908, Pepsi-Cola became one of the first companies to use motor vehicles in the delivery of goods, replacing the horse.
• To support efforts in World War 2, Pepsi had changed the color of the bottle caps from the third green red, white and blue (blue). The Pepsi canteen in Times Square - New York City for free cold Pepsi for more than a million families here to send messages to loved ones serving in the military are fighting overseas.• Actress Joan Crawford movie - wife of Alfred Steele, chairman of Pepsi has contributed in bringing the songs of Pepsi in the 40 years to become an advertising campaign in the 50s. She was chosen as board members after the death of Steele in 1959.
• In 1959, Soviet premier Nikita Krushchev and Vice President Richard Nixon Pepsi divide in the international trade fair in Moscow. Meeting the mass media in the United States notes with pictures thhich it "Krushchev becomes more friendly" - "Krushchev Gets sociable", like the slogan of the Pepsi ad in which time is "Be sociable, Have a Pepsi."
• In 1985, Pepsi launched a journey with a shuttle into space, carrying a specially designed "space can".

Branding strategy of Nike: "Just do it!"

Posters for the Nike brand was launched in 1988. Poster that shows Craig Blanchette - wheelchair racer famous American (wheelchair racing just for athletes with disabilities) - with strong words, brief, "Just do it!" (Roughly translated: "Be bold do you want!).

This strategy was ads Advertising Age magazine ranked the fourth assessment of the best ads of the 20th century, just behind the campaign of Volswagen, Coca-Cola and Marlboro. With this strategy Nike have hit on one of the main grave psychological importance of the U.S. rose to claim the will, the will to succeed, despite all obstacles.

Nike is the forerunner of Blue Ribbon Sports company, founded by Phil Knight in 1964, with the purpose of importing cheap sneakers Japanese brand in the U.S. market Onizuka. Knight was teamed with Bill Bowerman, a running coach at the University of Oregon, later to become experts designing the most innovative sports shoes for Nike, who contributed to the global Nike brand market production of sports shoes.

Blue Ribbons at the Sport Company having too many

problems. Brand name is forever struggling to keep selection, ranging from the Onizuka Onizuka Tiger, and Tiger and ASICs, is also the head is. Until 1972, the establishment of an independent product line in Korea, the new company Blue Ribbons Sport Nike decided on the name (the name of the Greek goddess of victory).

During the 1970s, Nike's sales jumped twice, even three times a year, from 14 million to $ 71 million in 1978, and $ 280 million in 1980, $ 900 million in 1983. In 1979, half the market for running shoes in the U.S. is controlled by Nike. The following year Nike surpass Adidas in the U.S. market.
The main reason for this success is due Nike outstanding grasp opportunities: the market for running shoes exercise left vacant since the mid-1970s. Both Adidas and Reebok do not pay attention to this market.
Phil Knight, Nike chairman, is a running track and field athletes Vietnam trip, so he quickly grasp the needs of the sports world. Knight's main undertakings during the construction of the Nike brand as high quality products will help athletes achieve higher performance in competition.
Mimicking the strategy of Adidas, Nike all the way to attract famous athletes involved in building a brand for yourself. Specific objectives are to be attached to using the Nike logo on the name of the winner and on television, a strategy to create an emotional attachment and psychological among consumers with the Nike brand through engagement with sports superstar.

But the image of the Nike sports superstars have different images of the Adidas Superstar. A sporting superstar Nike style to bold, even provocative, to show independence and originality.

The biggest success of Nike's marketing campaign probably figured out the character Michael Jordan as "human shields" for their brands. Jordan, the legendary superstar basketball world in the village, have contributed to the Nike brand to peak today, as he focused the entire personality of a superstar that Nike needed.

Immediately released Nike basketball shoes, Air Jordan (possibly temporary service "style Jordan"), and first year sales have reached more than $ 100 million. When Jordan shoes to play, he was the National Basketball Association American objections, prohibited as contrary to the provisions brought by the association.

Immediately get hold of this golden opportunity, immediately launched a Nike ad campaign with the phrase "Air Jordan banned because fashion design is full of it revolutionary." Massive media to protest the ban on unjustified said. National Basketball Association to surrender, to withdraw the ban again.

Has never been a campaign like this successful. Perhaps the most poignant because Adidas is the technical expertise to create the first Air Jordan shoe by a patent engineer and proposed sale to Adidas but the company refused to buy. This engineer was transferred to the Army for Nike.

Of course an important contribution in building the Nike brand is advertising. A program for advertising on television viewers watch the reporter Jordan is launching his hand up to hit the ball with the headline: "Who says humans can not fly?". This image became the symbol of the legendary talents of Jordan and posters from the most popular for this superstar.

Nike established in 1992 for "Nike City" (Niketown) on North Michigan Avenue in Chicago. In the branding strategy, this is the first unique initiative of Nike. In a land with total area of about 70,000 square feet, a three-story buildings dominate prance, divided into 18 booths displaying all Nike brand products.

Most importantly in this world Nike, the slogan "Be bold do you want" and "clam-visual life" is reflected in the visuals are great. There's even a sacred power for superstar Michael Jordan, but the "believers" can come here to show our devotion. People visit is covered in a sea of music is very exciting, arousing, replayed footage of the important sports competitions, and the middle space is gigantic picture of Jordan is "flying ".

1996 "Nike City" is the most attractive tourist spots of the city of Chicago with more than 1 million visitors and annual retail sales of 25 million.
How wise that Nike did not forget to exploit a potential

market in the 1980s: athletic shoes exclusively for women. This mistake just like ten years ago, Adidas has been indifferent to the running shoes market and mortification to see his face through the Nike case.

Reebok brand shoes ranked third after two elder Adidas and Nike, do not miss the opportunity, immediately launched sports shoes for women wanting to be upper class "fast chatter" a little bit. Female stars Cybill Shepherd wore a pair of Reebok shoes to attend the Emmy ceremony. Reebok's sales soared from $ 35 million in 1982 to $ 300 million in 1985. Nike shocked, storehouses filled with goods not sold, sales and profits plummeted, Phil Knight withdrew not directly run the company anymore, staffing cuts began.

There are many reasons for this, but the main reason is the "first pitch" massive Reebok. Through to the 1990 sale new Nike standing up when re-positioning its brand in the sports shoe market and health policy should not be free to invest in the field of fashion shoes.

Nike's secret of success is built upon the brand's emotional bond with consumers that their superstar fans. Identical shoes Jordan shoes that were brought during the game, then nothing "was" even more? Since then Nike decided to invest more heavily in recruiting the basketball superstar of the school.

Over the past 20 years, Nike has invested most of their advertising budget to cover the ground more than 2,000

Vietnamese athletes run wild. More than half of athletes in the National Basketball Association of America signed a contract for Nike ads.

But after being down Reebok "knocked" in the market of sports shoes for women, Nike decided to concentrate his forces on the stars selected without taking on too much. Jordan is the symbol of this change in brand strategy for Nike. Revenues began to thrive again. In 1986, Nike sales reach $ 1 billion. In 1990 this figure jumped to 2.2 billion, 3.8 billion in 1994, and 9.6 billion in 1998.

The main strategy of the Nike brand in this period focused on three borders of the nose: to build a brand around the basketball superstar Michael Jordan, using ad networks across the country to create an overwhelming presence of Nike brand in all places, systems development "Nike City" based on the idea of providing customers a unique experience and very focused, "living in space Nike, Nike sound, look Nike found everywhere. " It is not the word when told that Nike has improved branding strategy to a new level that competitors can rarely be reached.

Rolex watches - the symbol of nobility.

Available on the market in 1945, Rolex Oyster Datejust is the first time automatically became a symbol of nobility. Most of Rolex products are made by hand to ensure quality control.

rushing in 1914, when Prince Ferdinand of Austria shot blast, pushing the world into the bloodiest war in history, the Hans Wilsdorf founded the Bavarian company Rolex in London. At that time, Hans Wilsdorf decided to send their products to the Observatory in Switzerland to test and verify the accuracy

Rolex watches.

This is considered a right decision since then has become a brand Rolex watches in the world's first certified accuracy. And also very timely - outbreak of World War I, soldiers were required to watch a precise operation even more convenient because they must type pocket watch while working in the trenches.

Wilsdorf realized that the accuracy is the key brand values should always promote their properties on whenever possible. When Mercedes decided Gleitze will become the first woman to swim across the English Channel in 1926, Wilsdorf this immediately gave her a watch brand Rolex Oyster latest styles, to help her keep track of time while the excess sea. This event have created a valuable public franchise is on the rise.

If accuracy is a key to the success of the Rolex, the creativity is the key breakthrough Monday. In 1931, copyright registration Rolex watches on the first eternal seconds, which means side-winding watches no longer needed. In 1945, it became the first watch with date window noted. After that, the company also makes another breakthrough as the first dive watch, watch recorded with two different time zones at first

The main innovation together with the successful development of the Rolex has made people see the brand's history is the history of the watch industry. Rolex Oyster have been carefully checked by the typical faces of the clock industry and to achieve the title "The clock of the century."
Rolex's success is not only based on the combination of quality and creativity, but also a more important factor is marketing. With a brand has always been true desire is to always exceed supply.

Worldwide, the ubiquitous retailer Rolex. But through the years, Rolex gradually reduce the number of retail outlets of their watches. Unlike other brands always wanted to expand their distribution channels increasingly larger, Rolex went the opposite way. When there are many agents selling Rolex watches are the consequences for increased automation and the title of the iconic Rolex increasingly firmly established.

People do not wear a Rolex because of its accuracy. They wear a Rolex to assert themselves and their social

position. It's a Porsche can always carry on hand and also demonstrates the value of such equivalence.
Buy Rolex is an investment decision never losses. Persistence and the widespread popularity has ensured that this was an easy sell watches in the world. With a brand can tell you the exact time to the second one, it's surprising that Rolex has one of the brand over time. By the very close relationship with the history of watches, Rolex brand will remain there until we no longer want to look at your wrist to see the hour.

The secret of success:
- Quality. Rolex has been completely focused on quality right from the first product of his wrist in 1908. They affirmed that quality by sending her to watch Swiss observatory to be tested and certified to be accurate.
- Distribution. Brand by limiting the stimulus distribution. Only some retailers may sell any new Rolex watches.

- The relationship with history. Not self-invented Rolex watches, but that's the brand was first popularized this type of clock. The company is also associated with important inventions in the history of watches, such as clocks up eternal seconds.

Toyota's secret of success.

When General Motors cuts salaries, dividend and interest subsidies to deal with loss, Toyota announced a successful business figures for 2005. Good quality, strict management and always "know who they know" the secret of success of Japanese car manufacturers.

Date 7 / 2, a car maker in Japan reported net profit of Q4 2005 increased 34% to $ 3.3 billion, global sales at $ 45 billion up 15% over the same period in 2004 . Meanwhile, GM announced $ 8.6 billion loss in 2005 and announced plans to cut 30,000 jobs and close 12 plants over three years, 2006-2008.

Go find the secret of success of Toyota's what leaders are U.S. auto industry

concern. On the macro level, making Toyota the first cause growing success lies in quality. That's what America has no rivals. Even with the American people, Toyota launch on a cold day is not much different than normal, but with the national car is the opposite. Confidence in the quality of the Toyota brand in consumer psychology can be quantified through the Camry when it was the best selling car in America, while the hybrid to attract the attention of most people at the auto show Detroit.
In addition, editors of popular magazines Automotive News, Ed Lapham, said that Toyota's success lies in strict management method. "They provide quality products to consumers, they do not affect the environment, without affecting the world. Besides, they

also build a community of solidarity within the company, "said Lapham.

The third cause of how to build business strategy and services firm foundation. Rob Lache analyst at Deutsche Bank estimate, on average, Toyota earned $ 4,000 more per vehicle than GM or Ford .. "When you can earn more money means you can provide more equipment and can strengthen brand value by category of products that do not match," Lache said.

Besides high quality, success with hybrids and the boom in sport utility segment SUV, Toyota increased its market share in the line of light trucks and passenger cars to rise to the GM, Ford in the U.S. market.

"Toyota does things that competitors such as America can not build the plant away from them. This will allow Toyota to expand U.S. influence in particular and North America in general. It's one of the advantages most now, "George Magliano, an analyst at Global Insight said. That is Wednesday.

The success helped Toyota establish a new limit on the world auto market. Market leader in the world's No. 2 in Japan, there are some important strategies in China and is now No. 2 in the large car market on the planet. Moreover, market shares in Europe also is one of Toyota's ambitions in the former by continent, Toyota is still overlooked.

Another advantage of this manufacturer Toyota is not affected by the high wage policy that rivals the U.S. is a headache to find ways to cope. Analysts said that U.S. carmakers have narrowed the gap compared with Toyota quality, but the gap remains large brands. So, Toyota continues to use that advantage to rise up and growing closer to world No. 1 position on sales of GM.

The secret of success of the German car manufacturer

Industry of German automakers are still advancements are steadily on the world auto market. No other country, besides Germany, could have up to four automobile manufacturers worldwide reputation. And despite the domestic price of labor is high, the automobile manufacturer is now focused on production in Germany.

4 automobile manufacturers whose names independent beyond the borders of Germany is Daimler Chrysler, BMW, Volkswagen (VW) and Porsche. And all four companies are being very bright prospects in the process

of economic globalization. What is the success of the German car company?

Rationalization of production processes.

In Japan, the heyday of the automobile industry over the remaining two only Honda and Toyota is maintaining its independence. Mazda has now belong to "empire" Ford. Suzuki, Subaru and Isuzu became a subsidiary of General Motors. Controlled by Renault and Nissan from Daimler Chrysler to cut funding immediately, the Mitsubishi is expected to have an uncertain future. Automotive industry in Sweden are also gradually dependent on the U.S. (as Ford's Volvo and Saab belongs Hu of General Motors). The unique brand of British (Jaguar, Land Rover, Mini, Aston Martin, Rolls-Royce, Bentley) have been sold to the German or American companies. Italy's other car manufacturers (Fiat, Lancia, Alfa Romeo, Maserati and Ferrari) are all battling hard for their survival. France is one other European countries is still strong enough to keep two car brand is world class with Renault and PSA Group Peugeot and Citroen both brands.

In this context, the new look over the German's success seems surprising. Despite the globalization process, despite the continuous production have opened branches in South Africa, Eastern Europe, the production stage the most important details of the car is the car as the Daimler Group Chrysler, BMW and Porsche keep in water. Although accepted to pay higher labor costs and the weekly working time is short, but the German car manufacturers still see prospects for success. The cause lies in the fact that they know rationalizing production processes to create competitive with rivals in countries with lower production costs. As a result of labor productivity are very high and wage costs are 20% lower than production costs.

Technology investments.

German market is never interested in the protection of domestic products, such as Italy, which always limit the amount of annual import cars from Japan. But while government creates protected areas for Fiat cars, the car company is not promoting or improving vehicle technology development, respectively. The German car manufacturers have struggled to escape from problems similar to a confrontation with competitors coming from Asia.
In competition with the suffocating pressure, the German manufacturers have little hope to compete on price with other manufacturers in Japan and Korea. Their only chance lies in adding value for customers: the advantages of technology, increase safety and vehicle control easier. So the company decided to invest to develop new technologies. More than one third of the entire budget German automobile industry are spent on research and development stage products. Three most important improvements to enhance safety of vehicles made by German engineers coordinate with other providers offer: anti-theft system (ABS-anti-lock braking

systems), airbags and electronic protection program (ESP-electronic stability program).

The competition between the German car brand closer to the competition between regions based firms are Stuttgart, Munich and Wolfsburg. Three areas situated less than 100 miles apart, so it's easy to understand if the company always follow each other to learn new styles and techniques. Of course, this competition makes everyone benefit.

Putting customers' needs in the medium and long term strategies.
The German car manufacturers have a huge competitive advantage because they satisfy the requirements of customers for a fairly long period of time. They try to survive and endure billions of dollars of investment for new products and accept it may take up to three years to find markets.
The decline of American automobile manufacturers for several years has led to the common shareholders to consider very carefully the final result. If the number of cars sold decrease too much, managers often have to bear a greater pressure from shareholders and they immediately think of having to cut investment costs for new designs. But the cost cutting and financial mechanisms remain poorly just makes even more difficult financial stress. The problem is not solved and therefore can not prevent the decline of the company's momentum. Because of this reason that Ford had to lose the opportunity to become a leader. American car company

had acquired many brand giants such as Jaguar, Land Rover and Aston Martin. They did not spare money to invest, but because they can not quickly recover in the short term profit and the principal business activities are not effective as expected, the budget should be cut immediately. The new design is postponed or cut and Jaguar can forget my dream is to overthrow Mercedes-Benz in the European market.

Unlike the U.S. carmaker, the German carmaker is often less pressure from the stock market. Major shareholders are interested in trying to cooperate to make the company competitive. At BMW, Quandt family owns nearly 47% stake. At VW, the government holding 20% stake in Saxony, Deutsche Bank up 10% stake in Daimler Chrysler, Porsche and Piech families share each owns Porsche. The German car company understands that it is not accidental that the automobile manufacturer is now the most successful, Toyota, has a platform based on the most loyal shareholders, enabling them to focus on long-term goals .

Competitive strength to do so.

Assuming all four German car companies merged into a "German Motor Group", they will easily become a leader in this field. In the past there has been proposed to build the company into a unified block. The merger of Daimler and Benz in 1926 will probably be followed by many others, if not intervene at the last minute.

In the mid-'50s, the head of VW has signed a record with the CEO of Daimler-Benz. Accordingly, the two companies will reduce the level of competition in the areas of unnecessary and concentrate production of its traditional line of vehicles, particularly cars Volkswagen-name is also the corporate name will produce car- for the popular classes and Mercedes will produce vehicles for the elite. In 1965, VW announced a merger plan and see it as the only hope of survival for both companies. But Deutsche Bank, a major shareholder of Daimler, which destroys the idea.

In the early 1990s, when trouble Porsche, Daimler-Benz company well for special attention. Still, Porsche and Piech families have agreed not to sell their shares. Niefer Werner, CEO of the company at the time, tried to focus investments to focus on reviving the company. Porsche is today one of its best profits in the automobile industry.

Anyway, all automobile manufacturers must turn to face the risk of splitting or merging. It seems a group of "DB-BMW-VW-P" or a similar coalition will stand on all the competition, which VW and Daimler-Benz has ever done. Results may not develop as Audi A8 cars, or Mercedes-Benz is not developed to the A-Class.

Actually showed the company after the alliance would become weaker. A mishmash of brands and a "giant" but at least the spirit of cooperation will not easily accept the administration of a particular board but here is a group of German carmaker ".

However, there are a few successful mergers. Or prompted many people to the merger between the companies of Karl Benz and Daimler Motor Company in 1926 as a shareholding company Daimler-Benz. By 1929, this company has created a record profit at that - to sell 7800 cars per year.

80 year brand Durex.

1929 am, the first manufacturer Durex and products marketed condoms and contraception become the leading manufacturer in this market with a series of breakthrough innovation does not stop.
Durex brand originated in 1915 when L. A. Jackson founded the London Rubber Company. Operating in a small room behind a cigarette manufacturing facilities in London, Jackson began trading tools "protection" in the barbershop, this may be considered a fairly bold action and new during that time. In 1929, Durex name, derived from the word DUrability, Reliability and Excellence, which was officially registered.
3 years later, the first manufacturer of Durex operation, focused technical innovations in rubber processing and application of these techniques produce the most advanced.

In 1939 marked an important event. The amount of supply of condoms from Durex Germany banned therefore had to increase production to meet the growing needs of the military. In 1950, the company was privatized and renamed the London International. In 1999, after the merger with Seton Scholl, SSL International plc born.

The 80 is one other important milestones in the history of Durex. When you understand that AIDS and other infectious diseases through sexual contact is a serious problem, demand began to rise and the role of condoms was quickly recognized by society. Before the shift in the perception of the community, the retail system is expanding rapidly and today is no longer surprised when someone caught selling condoms openly in pubs, supermarkets, gas stations or drugstore anymore. Most recently, Durex expand distribution to the Topman clothing store, so the brand Durex can be exposed to many more young consumers with a message about safe sex life and healthy.

During its operation, Durex is committed to always ensure quality and makes for a healthy sexual relationship with contraceptive methods and prevention of diseases spread through sexual contact. Durex continued focus on improving the most modern techniques, including the best rubber formula, and scientific research. These improvements help customers of Durex sex life can be harmonious and healthy also helps Durex brand is growing stronger in the market.

According to statistics, every two seconds a person in Britain to buy a packet of condoms. With the majority of condoms sold are brand Durex, the Durex brand is obviously leading the market with 55 million units sold in the UK and own more than one billion units worldwide. Durex market share of more than twice the market share of competitors closely and evaluated their brand of condoms is leading.

Durex seeks to maintain and strengthen its leading position by improving awareness of healthy sexual life and safety. The majority of Durex activities geared to young people under the age of 16-24, giving the brand more customers will always be loyal to them throughout life.

In addition to developing the market, Durex is constantly expanding its market. The production of these products work to increase the excitement, the Durex market is also increasingly expanded. With products that stimulate the excitement as Sensation and Performa has created momentum for the emergence of Play, the first lubricating fluid, contributing to further relay the message of Durex and Durex helped to develop many new product next to a condom.

There are many variable factors to the manufacturer Durex condoms leading. First is the quality of Durex. In terms of innovation and technology, Durex always set the standard for quality and production rules strict. With priority on quality, Durex products must comply with the highest quality standards set by the company, and the stamp of quality is always a sign of Durex's most prestigious test.

In addition, Durex has launched research and new Durex handy design, create comfort and ease of use. Besides, also releasing Durex condoms with new technology, reducing the smell of rubber and plastic make the use of condoms is not a nuisance, more cumbersome. Next is the unique design of products such as Sensation and Pleasuremax, all kinds of scented condoms and of course, is the first Durex Performa with substance Benzocaine extends passionate moments.

Is the market leading companies in over 40 countries, the brand Durex dominant 26% market four billion condoms and contraception become the world's number one brand. In an effort to become an ambassador of sexual health community, both in terms of products as well as research, Durex brand has always been associated with safe sex issues in people's minds. So, this brand will continue to lead global markets for many years.

• The durable: Durable, reliable and always a perfect three main principles of operation of Durex.

• sense of responsibility: By-products of this brand is to contact the safety and sexual health, responsibility is not only a factor adding to the brand. Indeed, for Durex, the issue of corporate responsibility is a fundamental factor in their business. They not only combine the study of health and that the market and called for everyone's consciousness about the disease through sexual transmission.

Despite success no matter how they are still people who have changed the world . benefit to humanity than the success of the profits they are pioneers in the reform